Jesus
A Closer Walk

Jesus
A Closer Walk

Reflections on John 14-17
from the Edgar Cayce Readings

by William A. McGarey, M.D.

**ASSOCIATION FOR
RESEARCH AND
ENLIGHTENMENT**

A.R.E. Press • Virginia Beach • Virginia

A.R.E. Press
Sixty-Eighth & Atlantic Avenue
P.O. Box 656
Virginia Beach, VA 23451-0656

Library of Congress Cataloging-in-Publication Data
McGarey, William A.
    Jesus, a closer walk : reflections on John 14-17 from the Edgar Cayce readings / by William A. McGarey.
        p.   cm.
    ISBN 0-87604-409-7 (pbk.)
    1. Bible. N.T. John XIV-XVII—Miscellanea.   2. Cayce, Edgar, 1877-1945. Edgar Cayce readings. I. Cayce, Edgar, 1877-1945. Edgar Cayce readings. II. Title.
BS2615.5.M34   1998
226.5'06—DC21   98-12303

Cover design by Lightbourne Images

Contents

Preface

In 1971, inspired by the Edgar Cayce readings, a small
research group formed for the purpose of gathering, cor-
relating, and studying material on the Gospel of John.
Because of Cayce's particular emphasis on the fourteenth, fifteenth, sixteenth, and seventeenth chapters,
these came under close scrutiny.

It was a group effort from beginning to end, but the
result was a booklet entitled *A Closer Walk*. The research-
ers went through the readings and made preliminary selections, when possible, of eight to twelve extracts on a
given Bible verse. These selections then went to another

group who narrowed the choice down to four. These four excerpts were submitted for evaluation by the entire group who used the following questions as criteria:

How well does it amplify the Bible verse?

Could I apply it in my own life?

Could most others apply it in their lives?

In some cases fewer than four selections were available for a given verse. Where no extracts were available, an attempt was made to substitute a general reading, either on the Gospel of John or on a particular chapter. For purposes of comparative study, three translations of the Bible were used: the Authorized (King James) Version (A.V.), the Common Bible (C.B.), and the Jerusalem Bible (J.B.).*

Because their research of the Gospel of John was an ongoing project and by no means finished, the booklet was a purely informational offering and was not intended as a scholarly, in-depth study.

Thus, it was offered as a guideline and possible source of inspiration that might lead to a personal study of the Gospel of John and was in that manner lovingly presented by this dedicated group.

We sincerely thank the Gospel of John Research Group for their efforts in stimulating the minds of the readers of their booklet toward greater understanding of these four chapters. Their work provides the foundation for this present effort, which is presented with the hope that it might bring about an even deeper comprehension, a more profound recognition of the Christ, and thus another step might be made by each of us toward our goal to be one with the Creative Forces of the Universe.

William A. McGarey, M. D.

---

*Note: In this book, I will be using the New English Bible (N.E.B.) rather than the Jerusalem Bible, as the third translation of these four chapters.

Introduction

A Challenge to You, the Reader

If you had the opportunity to ask just one question of the Master, what do you think it would be?

Perhaps as we walk with the Christ through these four chapters of the book of John, that question will be answered.

The author of these chapters, the disciple John, was what we today would call a mystic, a seer. He wrote one of the four Gospels—the books of Matthew, Mark, Luke, and John—which document the birth, life, ministry, and death of Jesus.

The "beloved disciple," as he was known, touched into

the divinity of the Man Jesus in a way the other three disciples didn't. He was also the author of the Revelation of John, written on the isle of Patmos. It is a highly symbolic document which for two thousand years has defied efforts of biblical scholars to give it clarity and understanding for the reader.

Today, thousands—perhaps even millions—of individuals throughout the earth have reportedly had contact with Jesus in dreams, visions, or in face-to-face meetings in an altered state of consciousness. There are literally a multitude of other events, ranging from manifestations of the Mother Mary to the presence of angels in individual times of crisis, that are bringing the spiritual world closer to what we call the material dimension.

In my own experience, some of these events are not mysterious, but rather quite real. A group of us visited Medjugorje in what used to be Yugoslavia, in the late 1980s. Mary, mother of Jesus, had been appearing to six young people who psychically were given these visions and messages for their people over a period of several years, urging those who would listen to pray, repent, and love one another. Two members of our group reported seeing Mary as she appeared to one of these young people. Others had experiences beyond what we would call normal—seeing lights in the sky and hearing sounds, bells, thunder out of a cloudless sky—when Mary was to appear.

Six months later, I had a dream of Mary, as she was reported to have been seen by many. She was sitting—not standing—about eight or nine feet above the ground, on a little cloud, looking directly at me and smiling. She was sitting cross-legged, like a yogi, as if to be saying, "My messages are true, not only for these people and this religion, but for all those who dwell on the earth." There was nothing else in this very short dream, but, for me, it was very meaningful.

Books are currently available telling about how angels guard us, save us from disaster, bring us in ways often barely discernible into a greater awareness of our closeness to God. It's likely that out of any ten people you might talk to, you would find three or four who have had what they think is direct contact with angels at least once in their lives. I've had psychics tell me that my mother was my guardian angel for many years. She died when I was just seven years old, and she probably realized that I really needed someone to keep me out of trouble!

A close friend of mine was hanging a commercial sign many years ago when it came crashing down on top of him. He was saved from death or serious injury by an invisible force that removed him instantly from the danger spot to a place of safety. Events like these are truly common.

So-called near-death experiences (NDEs) are frequently reported by those experiencing them as including suddenly seeing the Christ or being enveloped in a wonderful loving light that they understand to be the Creator, God. These events have changed the lives of those who were thought to have died and then, through modern medical intervention, were brought back to the conscious world to tell their stories. Their faith was renewed, their fear of death eliminated, and they face the future with love and joy. They acknowledge that their lives will never be the same.

We are, indeed, living in a time when our spiritual life, our relationship with God, and our destiny as an eternal being tell us we need to awaken to reality. There is a God. There is a spiritual dimension, and we are here, lifetime after lifetime, on an adventure, a journey, to find our way back to a oneness with that Divine Being who brought us into existence.

Another man who has been called a mystic, a seer— Edgar Cayce—challenged us in his psychic readings to look at the fourteenth, fifteenth, sixteenth, and seventeenth chapters of John. In the process of his half a century or more of giving readings, Cayce pointed out to us that Jesus was not only talking to His disciples in these four chapters—He was actually speaking to each one of us, for we are all His children, in a way that we find difficult to understand. What an idea! Have we really looked deeply into what Jesus was saying in these last discourses with His disciples? Therein lies our challenge. In many of his readings, Cayce quoted portions of these sermons, these discussions, as he gave aid to those who were seeking help from his readings.

From the over 14,000 readings given by this man, Edgar Cayce, comes the story that we are truly eternal beings, having lived lifetime after lifetime, purposefully trying to find ourselves and find our way to a oneness with God.

I think it is obvious that if God created us in His image, then we have a right to know at a deeper level what Jesus was saying—what His promises were, what they are, and what they mean today.

I have many questions, and my beliefs center around Jesus and His Father. Many others in the varied environments in the world today have questions, also, that are still unanswered. We are all searching for an elusive goal that seems right, that seems true and eternal, whether we realize it or not. For the spiritual realm is as yet a mystery, an enigma. We can start this journey productively, however, by claiming that we truly do believe God exists and did create us in His image. No one can disprove that, and we always have the opportunity to believe or not to believe.

So let's take a walk with Jesus. Let's hear His voice—as John, the mystic, heard it and as Cayce, the mystic, expanded on it—so it might give us another perspective of what life is all about, another understanding from the

Source of all life itself. Perhaps the question you wanted to ask of the Master will be answered.

1

The Start of Our Journey

Before I entered medical school in 1943, I had planned to become a Presbyterian minister. In choosing medicine, I thought I had changed my direction. But it was only twelve years later, while practicing medicine in 1955, that I discovered the mysteries and wonders of the Edgar Cayce readings. In these readings, I recognized a concept that was not taught in medical school—that healing was not just of the body but rather involved the mind, the will, the emotions, and the spiritual part—the soul—of each individual person on the face of the earth.

Edgar Cayce from childhood was a devoted student of

the Bible. When he was twelve, he started reading it through once for every year of his life, from beginning to end. After catching up, he followed his commitment until he died in 1945. For me, his readings complemented, augmented, and enhanced the meanings found in the Bible and reached into the depths of the Universal Forces themselves. He came to understand giving his readings as doing the Work of the Christ.

His words in those readings followed closely the sometimes archaic language of the King James Version of the Bible. It has been difficult for some who study the readings to understand exactly what he meant—his sentences were long and sometimes convoluted. When asked his meaning on occasion, he wasted no words, merely suggesting that the inquirer study the readings—that would provide the answer.

It became apparent to me over the years, as I studied and applied and came to understand the readings, that ministry and medicine were not, in my life, opposite points of the compass but rather companions along the way to the goals and the purposes my soul chose before I was born.

In a sense, then, the ministry—my love of the Bible and Jesus' teachings—grew and prospered in my unconscious mind. My career in the field of medicine and healing, however, with all the turmoils that accompany every search for meaning, occupied my conscious mind.

I found several things coming together in my life: (1) my faith in the Christ, (2) my commitment to work creatively in my professional capacity as a physician, and (3) my experiences in helping those who were searching for the healing that everyone innately knows is possible.

Somewhere along the way, I discovered these four chapters of the Gospel of John which became the subject of some very intensive research by those dedicated individuals who called themselves the Gospel of John

Research Group. The promises, the predictions, and the statements of fact coming through these discourses that Jesus had with His disciples really came to life for me as I studied this material.

It was not, however, just the 117 verses in the four chapters that created a major change in my life and in my teaching others along the path. It would not have been complete without the Cayce readings that pointed out consistently to the searcher that Jesus was really talking to all of us. It was a personal conversation that has meaning for every soul on the planet. He was really speaking to me, to you, and, truly, to all of us.

The fourteenth, fifteenth, sixteenth, and seventeenth chapters of St. John were special to Cayce in the consciousness of his readings. His seriousness in pointing out these four chapters as being highly significant in the lives of everyone is highlighted here:

> . . . use the promises that are thine from the study especially of the 14th, 15th, 16th and 17th of John. Let them be as words to *thee!* 1614-1

> . . . His promises are sure—"If ye abide in me, I will abide with thee." Walk then closer in the light of His promises that are given in the 14th, 15th, 16th and 17th of John. Know that these are spoken to thee in thine extremity, in thy seeking. And as ye seek ye find. 3250-1

> Not that these portions are to be merely memorized so that they may be repeated (though do this), but meditate upon their meaning as applying to self. See self as being spoken to in same. For, these apply to self . . . 2696-1

So, how do we go about making these readings about

one specific portion of the Bible more personal, more usable, more real in our lives? As we make our way through these four chapters, let's be creative with our minds. Let's look at things from a truly different perspective. Let's make an adventure out of it.

We ordinarily see the day's events as being a necessary part of our lives—preparing meals, paying our bills, getting enough sleep, keeping the family headed in the right direction, putting money in the bank, going to work, making sure we get the news on television, voting—all these things and more! That's our day-to-day pattern of living.

As we read through the different portions of this book, let's instead think of ourselves as being souls—our original state—as inhabitants of the spiritual realm. We were there before we were born into the earth, and we will return when we leave the earth plane. What we call the spiritual dimension is God's realm. He is eternal—there is not a time when He was not. He created you and me and the rest of the souls on the earth in His image. That makes us eternal. We simply occupy the earth environment in a body that encompasses the soul. We are really quite different from what we usually think we are.

What does all that mean? First of all, of course, it means we must—from that perspective—look at things differently. It doesn't matter, for instance, if the rent is paid, as Cayce would say. We are more valuable to the Creative Forces of the Universe than even the earth itself, which we call our home. As souls, we must one day realize how much potential lies within this body of ours and how closely we are related to the Universal Force that we call God.

However, we also need to remember that we, as souls, have been in and out of the earth many times, searching, ever searching, for our destiny. The search, the adventure, takes us through many lifetimes—a divine plan that has come to be called reincarnation.

If these readings and the biblical references are correct, we were around when the earth was created and will still be here when the earth is rolled away as a scroll—eternal beings!

To look at things, then, from a different perspective, we might see ourselves reading this material from an eternal, spiritual, Godlike perspective—from the viewpoint as from the heavens, perhaps.

If we accept this perspective, however, we would be called upon to fulfill our purpose by putting into action in the earth the concepts we perceive from the point of view of that heavenly realm. In other words, there are only two laws we need to fulfill in this earth dimension: (1) love God, and (2) love our fellow human beings. This needs to be done here, in the earth (in this incarnation, if we choose), as we wrestle with the bills, the meals, the work, the relationships that we encounter in the environment we have chosen to experience.

So we might say that we reach up to the heavens to understand the nature of this spiritual journey we are taking and then look around us to put into action that portion of love we have come to understand. In a real sense, it is an adventure in spiritual consciousness in a material world.

We might be more comfortable with this kind of an adventure if we were to look more deeply into the reality of the world we live in, for it is not solid. It is, rather, made up of energy, of atoms that are miniature solar systems and universes in themselves, held together to create an environment where we can learn.

Learn what? As already indicated—learn how to love God and our fellow human beings. And then *do* it.

The next four chapters will be the site of our search, the place where we take that walk with Jesus. I may comment here and there, ask questions, and offer insights as we explore some of the promises that Jesus made, some of His predictions, concepts, understandings, and statements.

The selections from the readings which added so much to the richness of the original booklet are retained, of course. But I will quote from other Edgar Cayce readings where it appears to be helpful.

Through overcoming the earth, Jesus exists throughout the spiritual realm and is waiting to be invited into the very depths of that temple that has been prepared within our physical bodies. He belongs there, for He has indicated that we are gods in the making, and we are on our own journey to make that promise a reality through a oneness with Him.

Here, in these four chapters from the Gospel of John, Jesus is talking directly to you and to me! It's a challenge, and it is your choice to read or not to read. If you choose to go with it, then I challenge you to take those actual steps that lead you to your destination—to walk with Jesus through forests and fields as yet unexplored, asking Him those questions that you would love to have answered if He were here in body and you had that opportunity.

2

The Gospel of John, Chapter 14

"Let not thy heart be troubled; ye believe in God, believe also in Him—who is able to quicken the life as it flows through thy body, thy mind, thy soul . . . " (2448-2)

This is the first of four discourses that Jesus had with His disciples. It was during the Last Supper, when Judas left the group, that Jesus saw that the time was near for the Romans to seek Him out and put Him in jail. He had told the disciples that He was going to a place where none of them could now follow. As Jesus was washing Peter's feet, Peter said to Jesus in his characteristic forthright manner, "I will lay down my life for you!" Then came the famous response as Jesus told Peter, "I tell you in very truth, before the cock crows you will have denied me three times."

Then He proceeded to tell the eleven who were left, "Set your troubled hearts at rest. Trust in God always; trust also in me." It was in reference to the beginning of the fourteenth chapter that Edgar Cayce suggested that Jesus was telling you and me, in effect, that these promises fashioned some two thousand years ago and given to His disciples are for all of us who love God and are committed to love one another.

What does it mean to you, for instance, to "Set your troubled hearts at rest"? Think for a moment. When events in one's life bring trouble into one's consciousness, one's heart, there is need for a change to bring rest to one's soul. And the change is often difficult to recognize as being valuable, masquerading instead as mental or physical pain, emotional turmoil, or even sickness of the physical body. Yet it was meant for the disciples and is meant for us today as soul growth along the path to a oneness with God.

We do not know, of course, what exists in the consciousness of another person, so we are left with an unanswered question when we look at another human being and wonder if that one is trying to find rest for a troubled heart. Or is the person still in rebellion—unable to let go?

These were the tenets and truths of that experience. Hold fast to them in thy daily walks through life. Not that disturbing periods do not come, as well as periods of material benefits, and also periods of hate and strifes arising among those about thee; but know in whom and in what thou hast believed, and know the author of thy faith, and ye will find it answering within self. For *there*, as ye were taught then, *He* will meet thee; thy Savior, thy God—in thine own temple. For thy body is the temple of the living God. Keep it in such ways and

manners that ye may always entertain Him there.
Not offering strange fires of hate, strange fires of
jealousy, strange fires of dissension; but love, which
is the oil of salvation, which is the way of truth and
light! 2073-2

We know that life is an ongoing stream of consciousness. We change with each lifetime, placing in the care of
our unconscious minds the events that need to be
looked at again, sometime in the future. Then our parents, whom we have chosen, teach us their way of looking at things, their perspective on life, and we only
awaken to a portion of the totality of what we have built
in the past, as we grow older and search for our destiny
and try to awaken to what God wants us to do.

Let's start this chapter, then, believing that we really
are created in the image of God, eternal beings, trying to
find our way back to what was our original state—the
destiny which has always been there from the beginning.

Let's look for the promises, the concepts, the nuggets
of wisdom and of love that are hidden in some of these
readings, some of these verses—some that won't be
elaborated on. For the richness of these selections is
sometimes beyond the reach of our conscious minds.

John 14:1

**Set your troubled hearts at rest. Trust in God al-
ways; trust also in me. (N.E.B.)**

**Let not your heart be troubled: ye believe in God,
believe also in me. (A.V.)**

**Let not your hearts be troubled; believe in God,
believe also in me. (C.B.)**

Let not thy heart be troubled. For He careth for thee. Would that all would come to know, "Jesus careth for me." If that is held constantly in the trials of the day, in the troubles of associations or activities, there need be little fear or doubt. Then, do with thy might what thy hands find to do day by day. For the Lord, the Christ who came, who will save the world—careth for thee. 262-128

As has been well said, let not your heart be troubled. Ye believe in God. Then believe in that closeness with which ye may walk with the Master. For as He has said, "If ye open the door I will enter." But when there is considered only self, self's anxieties, self's fears, these cause the closing of that freedom with which the Master may speak with thee. 1695-4

Let not thy heart be troubled; ye believe in God, believe also in Him—who is able to quicken the life as it flows through thy body, thy mind, thy soul, to a full regeneration in the material world, then hope in the mental, then truth in the spiritual. For, He *is* truth, and the light, the way; that each soul may find the way from the darkness back to God—even as He. 2448-2

Thou hast seen and heard how that "My Spirit beareth witness" in the experience of those that seek to do His biddings, who would make of themselves channels that the glory of the Father may be manifested through the Son and those that have loved His ways.
Then, trouble not thine self that there are those things in the material that would make for dissension and for trouble in the body, in the mind. Put

thy trust rather in those things that are revealed in thy experience. For, these be they that will make thee more and more aware of "My Presence" in the earth. Be not overcome of those evil influences that are abroad, but rather give place to those things that will strengthen and sustain thee. 378-33

John 14:2

There are many dwelling-places in my Father's house; if it were not so I should have told you; for I am going there on purpose to prepare a place for you . . . (N.E.B.)

In my Father's house are many mansions: if it were not so, I would have told you. I go to prepare a place for you. (A.V.)

In my Father's house are many rooms; if it were not so, would I have told you that I go to prepare a place for you? (C.B.)

. . . "In my Father's house are many mansions"— many consciousnesses, many stages of enfoldment, of unfoldment, of blessings, of sources. And yet God has not willed that any soul should perish, but has with every temptation, every trial, prepared a way of escape—or a way to meet same; which is indicated here by the Creator, the Maker of heaven and earth and all that in them be. 2879-1

In thy mind and heart are many possibilities, many opportunities. Lose not a single one to make known the love that the Master has for the children of men. For He, too, was one of them. So in thy ways of grace and mercy, show forth the Lord's death, the

Lord's life, the Lord's love, until He comes again.
5758-1

In thy Father's house are many mansions. All are
not for the one nor the other; each according to the
use of his abilities is meted that with which he is
attuned. Keep thy purposes then, keep thy aims, thy
desires, of a material, of a mental, of a spiritual nature, attuned to that *you* would occupy . . . forever.
For these temporal things must pass away, but that
spiritual house, that temple—that cleanliness so
akin to godliness—is that which lives on and on. It
ever was, and you have drawn close to His ways.
Then steer thy course to that thou knowest that
brings peace, and the calm that brings happiness
in thy daily life. 262-109

In thy searching, then, begin with reading each
day just a few verses of the 14th, 15th, 16th and 17th
of St. John. First read in the 14th, "In my father's
house are many mansions." Dwell on that, not for
an hour or a minute but for a day—as ye go about
your work. Who is your father? Whom does He
mean, in speaking to thee? And what does He mean
by mansions? and that there are many mansions in
His house? What house? It is indeed thy body, that
is the temple. Many mansions are in that body,
many temples. For the body has been again and
again in the experiences of the earth, and thus they
are sometimes mansions, sometimes huts, sometimes homes, and again they become those places
where we dislike to abide. 3578-1

John 14:3

And if I go and prepare a place for you, I shall come

again and receive you to myself, so that where I am
you may be also ... (N.E.B.)

And if I go and prepare a place for you, I will come
again, and receive you unto myself; that where I
am, there ye may be also. (A.V.)

And when I go and prepare a place for you, I will
come again and will take you to myself, that where
I am you may be also. (C.B.)

Promises—Do We Believe Them?

There are some amazing promises found throughout
these four chapters of the Gospel of John, and in the
readings Cayce often heightened our usual view of what
might be a reasonable understanding of these promises
and of how they may become part of our lives.

One promise, for instance, is that "[He] is able to
quicken the life as it flows through thy body, thy mind,
thy soul, to a full regeneration in the material world, then
hope in the mental, then truth in the spiritual." (2448-2)

Remember, our bodies are as temples where He will
meet us—where He *has* met us over these many incarnations. This promise talks about healing of our bodies,
a greater attunement than we usually can comprehend.
For, if the full force of Life expresses itself boundlessly
within the temple of our bodies, then life will manifest
as regeneration and healing of the body itself. As we recognize what is happening, then indeed there will come
about hope in the mind and an acknowledgment of truth
in the spiritual self, the soul.

The next question, of course, is "How do we get to that
point of knowing and recognizing the full flow of Life
within our beings?" The single answer, of course, is full
attunement with the Divine. But that takes time and is

probably what we have been searching for over our extended incarnations here in the earth. The practical answer is found in bits and pieces throughout the Bible and in these readings that Cayce gave. Jesus talked about the many mansions in His Father's house. In Cayce's perspective, the many mansions are many consciousnesses, many stages of enfoldment, of unfoldment, of blessings, of sources—truly many lifetimes. At another time, Cayce asked:

"Who is your father? Whom does He mean, in speaking to thee? And what does He mean by mansions? and that there are many mansions in His house? What house? It is indeed thy body, that is the temple. Many mansions are in that body, many temples. For the body has been again and again in the experiences of the earth, and thus they are sometimes mansions, sometimes huts, sometimes homes, and again they become those places where we dislike to abide." (3578-1)

But, in these chapters, we have another promise. A special place has been prepared for us—another consciousness that leads us toward a greater oneness with God. Is it an awareness of the presence of the Christ Consciousness? We have only the implied magnificence, not the details.

"Keep that body as the Temple of God. Supply it with all the beauties as ye would a physical service to Him that ye would honor most—in thy heart, in thy body, in thy mind, in thy purpose. And let it ever be with that spirit of truth as manifested in Him, 'I go unto the Father, that where I am ye may be also.' It may be thine now if ye will accept it . . . " (2794-3) Perhaps that special place may be ours *if* we keep the body as we would keep the Temple itself as a place of worship *and* if we simply *accept* the mansion as ours.

Too often we consciously think that we are pretty well organized and balanced and that we know these eternal messages, sometimes by heart. Yet, we still do not walk with the Christ daily—all the time—nor manifest all those fruits of the Spirit.

If we are to claim these promises as our own—whatever they may be—we need to fulfill the concept of doing with all our might what we find to do, wherever we are, in our home, with our spouse, in our business, among friends, even among enemies. Cayce said it like this: "And how canst thou claim them [the promises] unless ye in thine own knowledge, thine own consciousness, *have* done—do do from day to day—that thy heart has told and does tell thee is in keeping with what He has promised?" (5749-6)

Maybe we, in our quiet moments, seeking to know ourselves even as we are known by the Creative Forces, might wish to follow these instructions: How may we learn?

[By] Being able to, as it were, *literally,* stand aside and watch self pass by! Take the time to occasionally be sufficiently introspective of that, that may happen in self's relation to others, to *see* the reactions of others as to that as was done by self; for true—as it has been said—no man lives to himself, no man dies to himself; for as the currents run to bring about the forces that are so necessary to man's own in these material things, so are those forces in self active upon those whom we act upon. Being able, then, to see self as others see you; for, as has been given, "*Now* we know in part, then shall we know even as we are known." Then, in Him so let thy life be in Him, in thought, in deed, that "Ye that have known me have known the Father also" may be truly said of self. Stand aside and watch self pass by! 262-9

And, we might add—forget about our own welfare; keep our purposes, aims, and direction attuned to that place we would occupy. Always remember that He is talking to you and me—and we truly know how to get there. He is the Way, the Truth, and the Light, the Life.

What did He give as thy standard? "Inasmuch as ye do it unto the least of these, my brethren, ye do it unto me." Then, see rather in that thou wouldst give in word of mouth, in deed, in act of body, that thou art ministering unto thy Lord. For of such He said, "I will come again to you, and comfort you—I will receive you unto myself—I *will* abide with you." Art thou living in such an atmosphere? 262-64

But know that thy body is indeed the temple of the living God. And He has promised to meet thee. Keep that body as the temple of God. Supply it with all the beauties as ye would a physical service to Him that ye would honor most—in thy heart, in thy body, in thy mind, in thy purpose. And let it ever be with that spirit of truth as manifested in Him, "I go unto the Father, that where I am ye may be also." It may be thine now if ye will accept it . . . 2794-3

For as many as have named the name, and that do unto their brethren the deeds that bring to them (to you) that closeness, oneness of purpose with Him, may know—ye, too—in body, in mind, that He *lives today*, and will come and receive you unto Himself, that where He is there ye may be also.

Crucify Him not in thy mind nor in thy bodily activities. Be not overcome by those things that are of the earth-earthy. Rather clothe thy body, thy mind, with the thoughts, the deeds, the privileges that His suffering as a man brought to thee, that He indeed might be the first of those that slept, the first of those that came in the flesh, that passed through all those periods of preparation in the flesh, even as thou.

But if ye would put on Him, ye must claim His promises as thine own. And how canst thou claim them unless ye in thine own knowledge, thine own consciousness, *have* done—do do from day to day—that thy heart has told and does tell thee is in keeping with what He has promised? 5749-6

John 14:4

And my way there is known to you. (N.E.B.)

And whither I go ye know, and the way ye know. (A.V.)

And you know the way where I am going. (C.B.)

Success and Attunement

As human beings trying to wend our way through the sometimes turbulent activities of the material world, we often set our sights on being successful. Since success is frequently measured or determined by the kind of house we own or the stocks that we have accumulated, by the size of our bank account or the make or number of the cars that we drive, it becomes obvious that money is the means by which these things are obtained. Thus riches are often synonymous with success in this world.

Looking at success from the standpoint of one who is a native of the spiritual realm—a soul created by God, in His image—the material definition misses the mark. Cayce tells the story very clearly and with emphasis, bringing the Way and the element of success together in a unique manner:

Will ye put word by word, line upon line, precept
upon precept, here a little, there a little, a reminder
to all that they alone who love the Lord and His
ways and His precepts *shall* succeed? whether they
be in the position of affluence, in authority, or as
the servant? They alone shall succeed, now or hereafter!

For the way ye know, and the truth . . . needs *no*
verification, but thy glorification in thy life, thy
heart, thy manner of dealing with thy fellow man.
257-201

Then, what about attunement? Cayce told us that in
this manner may we know the way—"The manner *in*
which each may know they are *in* attune, is the ability to
feel that consciousness of the sincere desire *within* to *be*
a blessing, *a* channel, to someone." (281-3)

So it may be necessary for us to meditate much in order for us to be in attunement with the Divine. But it may
also be that when we *feel* the awareness of our deep desire within to be a blessing or a channel for blessings to
someone, that, too, is attunement.

It seems that there is a definite connection between
living one's beliefs and feeling the commitment of wanting to do something for another. To be a channel, to do
things constructively, that which we do, day by day, here
a little and there a little, spells success in God's eyes. It
doesn't necessarily have anything to do with how much
money we make or have put away.

In this manner may ye know the way; for, as has
been given, "I go—and the *way* ye know." The manner in which each may know they are *in* attune, is
the ability to feel that consciousness of the sincere
desire *within* to *be* a blessing, *a* channel, to someone. 281-3

Keep, in thine meditations, that of the *Christ* Consciousness being magnified *in* thee day by day. So *will* this cast out fear, that becomes a stumbling block at times to thine *own* endeavors; for we—humanlike—so *easily* forget the promise, that "If ye abide in me, I will *abide* in thee," and "What ye ask in *my* name, *believing*, ye shall have. The way ye know, for as I go to the Father and abide in Him and ye in me, so *is* the Father *magnified* in the earth *through that* promise as is kept by thee *in* me day by day." 1742-4

He that walketh in the light, and purposes in his heart to *do, be,* that which *the* Creative Forces would *have* one be, shall *not* be *left* alone! for though he walk through the valley of the shadow of death, His arm, His hand, will direct thy ways. His rod, His staff, will comfort thee! Though they walk through green pastures, or in the ways that lead down to the sea, yet His Spirit, His arm, His face, will *comfort* thee in the *way* thou goest! When one, then, is so guarded, so guided, *indeed* for a *purpose* is one kept in the way! Be not unmindful of the necessity, then, that He that guideth shall *show* the way! *Do not* attempt with thine short hands, thine poor vision, thine hardened heart, thine encasement in *this* sphere, to not give the credit where *credit* [is] due, nor censure where censure is due. Rather let thy yeas be yea, and thy nays be nay; for the way ye know, the *manner* ye know! *Do not* tempt the Lord, thy God! 1909-3

John 14:5

Thomas said, Lord, we do not know where you are going, so how can we know the way? (N.E.B.)

Thomas saith unto him, Lord, we know not whither thou goest; and how can we know the way? (A.V.)

Thomas said to him, Lord, we do not know where you are going; how can we know the way? (C.B.)

Let not thy heart be troubled; ye believe in God, believe also in Him—who is the way, the truth and the light.

Let thy heart and mind be set on those trusts He has put in thee, and upon the promises of the abiding spirit in and with thee. 2683-1

John 14:6

Jesus replied, I am the way; I am the truth and I am life; no one comes to the Father except by me. (N.E.B.)

Jesus saith unto him, I am the way, the truth, and the life: no man cometh unto the Father, but by me. (A.V.)

Jesus said to him, I am the way, and the truth, and the life; no one comes to the Father, but by me. (C.B.)

He Is the Way

The way to Los Angeles from Phoenix is due west on Interstate 10. Unfortunately, knowing that doesn't get us to Los Angeles unless we move—by plane, car, or some manner of transportation—far enough to reach our destination.

It's like that when our mind accepts and comprehends that Jesus is the Way. It does us no good unless our "mind dwells upon the fruit of the spirit—faith, hope, gentleness, kindness, patience—[then] it may blossom into that which brings the hope of man, the confidence in his brethren, the faith in his God." (2629-1)

However, before we might be the Way for another soul who is seeking, we have to move our bodies by living, in relationship with others, these same fruits of the Spirit. To hold to one idea and put another into practice divides us and leads us in the wrong direction. I've been told, "Your actions speak so loud, I can't hear what you say."

We might say, then, in order to complete our soul journey, we need to travel in the same path, the same way, that Jesus traveled. We need to love each other, even our worst enemy, for God dwells within that person, too, no matter how far one has deviated from one's soul nature. And we need to love and accept our own self. By doing these things—being patient when someone fails to function the way he or she has been instructed, forgiving that loved one, no matter how he or she has acted—we put the fruits of the Spirit into action. They can only be part of us if we live them moment by moment.

It's really not so difficult; for, while He manifested love in every action, with a child or an erring parent or disciple, He also showed us that this Way is the lighted path; it is love; it is light. He is light. He is there to help us every step of the way (see reading 2031-1 below).

The peace that comes from Him comes only by abiding in His word. What, then, is His word? Put away those things that would cause fear or doubt. *Know* in thy inner self that He *is* the way, the truth, the light. There is no other joy to compare with the joy which comes from being counted worthy of His recognition, and the knowledge that in His way ye abide day by day. 262-128

Then, search ye the Scriptures; for in them ye will

find security, contentment, peace, harmony—as ye pattern thy thoughts, thy purposes, thy desires, after Him who is the way, the truth, the light. For He hath gone the whole way, and hath promised, "Believe in me, and I—abiding in thee—will bring that to pass in thy experience that brings peace; not as the world gives peace, but that which is safe in the knowledge of thy relationships to thy fellow man." 2031-1

Hence, as He indicated, each soul should be aware that while the material motives must be within, to keep harmony in the body and in mind they must be in accord with the Way. He *is* the way, the truth, the ideal.

Then, let not any influence or purpose sway the entity from holding to and declaring the purpose *in* body, *in* mind that none other than He may direct. 1947-8

And know today there is no other than that found in the admonition given by Jesus of Nazareth, Jesus the Christ—"If ye believe in God, believe also in me." Hence He is that to which the mind of the individual entity responds. He is the way, the mind is the way. And as the mind dwells upon the fruit of the spirit—faith, hope, gentleness, kindness, patience—it may blossom into that which brings the hope of man, the confidence in his brethren, the faith in his God. 2629-1

John 14:7

If you knew me you would know my Father too. From now on you do know him; you have seen him. (N.E.B.)

If ye had known me, ye should have known my Father also: and from henceforth ye know him, and have seen him. (A.V.)

If you had known me, you would have known my Father also; henceforth you know him and have seen him. (C.B.)

Take the time to occasionally be sufficiently introspective of that, that may happen in self's relation to others, to *see* the reactions of others as to that as was done by self; for true—as it has been said—no man lives to himself, no man dies to himself; for as the currents run to bring about the forces that are so necessary to man's own in these material things, so are those forces in self active upon those whom we act upon. Being able, then, to see self as others see you; for, as has been given, "*Now* we know in part, then shall we know even as we are known." Then, in Him so let thy life be in Him, in thought, in deed, that "Ye that have known me have known the Father also" may be truly said of self. Stand aside and watch self pass by! 262-9

. . . "Ye that have known me knoweth my Father also, for I am in Him, and ye in me may know that love that maketh the life burn as an ember in a darkened and unregenerated world. For unto me must come all that would find the way. I *am* the way. Ye are my brethren. Ye have been begotten in the flesh through the love made manifest in the earth."

Then, in the spirit and in the mind that hast brought thee to that understanding and consciousness of His love made manifest, abide ye day by day. 262-44

John 14:8

Philip said to him, "Lord, show us the Father and we ask no more." (N.E.B.)

Philip saith unto him, Lord, show us the Father, and it sufficeth us. (A.V.)

Philip said to him, "Lord, show us the Father, and we shall be satisfied." (C.B.)

"Me ye have known, and the way ye know, for I am the way, the truth, and the light. Had ye not known me ye would not have known the Father, but seeing me, in me ye see the Father also. If I go not away the spirit will not come unto you, but I go to the Father, and the spirit will *abide* with you and bring to your *remembrance* all things whatsoever I have said unto you." These—this, mine son—and thou wilt see, even in the counsel of thine own hearts, as men, *this* fulfilled in the street, in the market place, or in thine *own* home. 137-123

John 14:9

Jesus answered, "Have I been all this time with you, Philip, and you still do not know me? Anyone who has seen me has seen the Father. Then how can you say, 'Show us the Father'?" (N.E.B.)

Jesus saith unto him, Have I been so long time with you, and yet hast thou not known me, Philip? He that hath seen me hath seen the Father; and how sayest thou then, Show us the Father? (A.V.)

Jesus said to him, Have I been with you so long, and

yet you do not know me, Philip? He who has seen me has seen the Father; how can you say, "Show us the Father"? (C.B.)

For He is life, and the author of same; yet He offers Himself as a way in which ye may approach that throne of grace and mercy in the loving Father—about whom He has told thee! He has shown thee the Father by the manner in which He presented Himself.

Then, open thy heart, thy mind, that thy body and thy service and thy activities before thy fellow men may indeed be as the beauty of the opportunities that lie before thee in thy relationships to others. 1632-2

. . . "He that hath seen me hath seen the Father also," and as this is applicable in this life as given, who made self of no estate that others might have an access, and He becoming the Advocate through which the approach may be made by the life as man lived in the earth plane, so we in passing through the earth plane may make our individual lives so one with the Father that we may make the guiding, the advocate of others with the Father. 900-65

John 14:10

Do you not believe that I am in the Father, and the Father in me? I am not myself the source of the words I speak to you; it is the Father who dwells in me doing his own work. (N.E.B.)

Believest thou not that I am in the Father, and the Father in me? the words that I speak unto you I speak not of myself; but the Father that dwelleth

in me, he doeth the works. (A.V.)

Do you not believe that I am in the Father and the Father in me? The words that I say to you I do not speak on my own authority; but the Father who dwells in me does his works. (C.B.)

. . . if that ye have heard, that ye have seen, that ye have experienced, that ye have pondered in thine heart makes of thee a better father, a better mother, a better friend, a better neighbor, more gentle with those that are cross, more loving to those that are dishonest, more patient with those that storm here or there, then ye are experiencing the true Knowledge of the Father.

If it has brought not this, if it brings not in thine own experience the fruits of the Spirit, then it is not of God; neither is it countenanced by thy Brother, thy Savior, who prayed that He might, that ye might, that all men everywhere might be of the one mind *in God!* 262-97

Did He find fault?

Do ye? Did He question purposes? Do ye? Do ye love those who hate thee? He did. Do you keep the words, "Not of myself but my Father who worketh in and through me" as thy ideal? He did. He is thy pattern. That is thy protection ever. For it is in Him ye live and move and have thy being.

Ye know that—act like it! 2982-4

Know then that the force in nature that is called electrical or electricity is that same force ye worship as Creative or God in action!

Seeing this, feeling this, knowing this, ye will find that not only does the body become revivified, but by the creating in every atom of its being the knowledge of the activity of this Creative Force or Principle as related to spirit, mind, body—all three are renewed. For these are as the trinity in the body, these are as the trinity in the principles of the very life force itself—as the Father, the Son, the Spirit— the Body, the Mind, the Spirit—these are one. One Spirit, One God, One Activity. Then see Him, know Him, in those influences. For even as the Son gave, "I of myself may do nothing, but as the Father worketh in me, through me." So it is with an individual entity or soul that sees the activities which man hath been given in the earth. For the first command is ever as thine own, "Be ye *wise* and *subdue the earth.*" 1299-1

If thou art in Him thou art beyond being hurt, being tempted, being slurred at, being mistreated; for "Not of myself do I these, but the Father that worketh in me" gave He to those that would name Him as their access, their approach to presenting that soul that is in the image of the Maker safe to Him, for he that forgives much shall have much forgiven him, and he that beareth much in the body— through the raising in the Christ, in the Spirit, in the mind of the Christ—shall be like Him, one with Him. Thus shall the body use those things that have hindered, that would cause the quickness of the speech, the flush at being stepped upon, being athwarted in the wishes, the desires of self. Not *self* is it being done to; rather to the spirit of the God that is within each soul. When this is seen and understood then in self, there may come the greater joy in the knowledge that He, the Christ in thine mind, that building influence that makes for all those things that partake of Him and His associa-

tions with the Father, brings then to thine own experience, thine own awareness, that thy soul is one
with Him. 864-1

John 14:11

**Believe me when I say that I am in the Father and
the Father in me; or else accept the evidence of the
deeds themselves. (N.E.B.)**

**Believe me that I am in the Father, and the Father
in me; or else believe me for the very works' sake.
(A.V.)**

**Believe me that I am in the Father and the Father
in me; or else believe me for the sake of the works
themselves. (C.B.)**

Have You Seen the Father?

In working with patients in our residential program,
we—the patient and myself—have at times come close
enough to one another that I can ask this question:
"Have you seen the Father?" I could not have asked that
question of another unless I had pondered and formu-
lated to some extent my own answer.

My first attempt was simplified, but based on several
biblical concepts: God is Love; Hear, O Israel, the Lord
thy God is One God—One; God is a Spirit; Jesus and the
Father are One, and they dwell within our own bodies,
which are the Temples of God; the fruits of the Spirit are
gentleness, kindness, forgiveness, understanding—all
the many facets of love as Paul described in First
Corinthians, the thirteenth chapter, and in Galatians, the
fourth and fifth chapters.

These concepts must be related. Jesus lived love

throughout His lifetime, yet claimed that it was not He but the Father that moved in and through Him that did the works. Thus it was love manifested in the earth that accomplished all that Jesus did. Jesus also said that we could do all that He did. We could, then, show compassion for a person who is suffering. We could help another in distress. We could forgive our erring brother, sister, or friend. We could touch someone and bring healing to that one's body.

When we see another doing one of these simple acts of faith and joy and healing, we are seeing the Father. For it is love that brings all these things into being, and God is love.

I recall finding a Cayce reading that told *me*, certainly, that unless I could see God in the patient who is sitting opposite me in the examining room, I had not even begun to grow. We see, but often we don't see. If, indeed, each of us was formed in the image of God, the Spirit of God dwells therein, and it is up to us to meet the challenge of seeing God in that individual. We must do it at some point in time. Why not now?

So, can you say that you have seen the Father? If you have, then "ye in me may know that love that maketh the life burn as an ember in a darkened and unregenerated world. For unto me must come all that would find the way. I *am* the way. Ye are my brethren. Ye have been begotten in the flesh through the love made manifest in the earth." (262-44)

As I have pondered how it is and when it is that I see the Father, I also have thought how remarkable it is that we have been able to discern at least a portion of the nature of our spiritual beings. Knowing that we have been in existence since before the very foundation of the earth as spiritual entities formed in God's image, we have moved away from God like the young man in the story of the prodigal son, forgetting from whence we came and where we are destined to go.

But we can say, "Yes, I have seen the Father, in the eyes of my mother who died painfully from cancer, and in the disappointed face of the friend who didn't understand that I was honestly trying to help."

These experiences become as soul growth for each of us and fill the world with just that much light as we minister to those about us. We can then know the reality of the statement, "Me ye have known, and the way ye know, for I am the way, the truth, and the light. Had ye not known me ye would not have known the Father."

> Study that thou sayest, that thou doest, and reserve *nothing*—in strength of body or mind—in service to others, *that* is a reflection of that He would have thee do, as thou knowest how. As was given by Him, let thine works, thine efforts, be even as was said by Him—"If ye will not believe me, ye *will* believe for the very works' sake—for the things I do bespeak *that* I believe I *AM!*" 262-12

> For the whole law, as He gave, is to love the Lord thy God with all thy heart, thy mind, thy body; thy neighbor as thyself.
>
> There is not looking then for the message to be descended from heaven by those that may be of this or that thought, but rather as He gave, "The kingdom of heaven is within—Believe thou in me—if not because of my existence because of the works that I do," that ye may do in Him; "for of myself I can do nothing, only as the Father worketh in me." 1158-14

> Then, let thy yeas be yea. Reason with, even as He did with His disciples, and may thy life be even as His, "If ye believe not for my words, believe for

the very works' sake." For, in His keeping will He bear thee up and direct thee in the ways thou shouldst go; for, as He has given in the bodies of many that they may bear in them the glorifyings not of other than those things that He has given in their keeping for the glorification of the Father's love to the sons of men, so may *thou* find—in that expression of love to thine own body, as found in this soul—that *He* may bless thee, may *keep* thee, and keep her in that way that leads to life everlasting in Him. 608-7

. . . there needs be that expression which might be interpreted even in the manner in which the Master gave to some of His close associates or disciples, "If ye believe me not because of me, believe for the very works' sake."

Then, that apply or make practical in thy activities with thy daughter—not by the physical sustenance or sustaining, though at times it requires just that, but by thy conversation, thy activity, thy dealings with others—yea, with all—in such measures as to be "for the very works' sake." 1472-13

John 14:12

In truth, in very truth I tell you, he who has faith in me will do what I am doing; and he will do greater things still because I am going to the Father. (N.E.B.)

Verily, verily, I say unto you, He that believeth on me, the works that I do shall he do also; and greater works than these shall he do; because I go unto my Father. (A.V.)

**Truly, truly, I say to you, he who believes in me will
also do the works that I do; and greater works than
these will he do, because I go to the Father. (C.B.)**

Belief or Commitment

Jesus said, "Believe me when I say that I am in the Father and the Father in me." (John 14:11) This may be a challenge because we do not know what He meant when He said, "Believe me." Today we have good dictionaries, but rather than clarifying, they often mystify and confuse us. *Believe,* for instance, is defined many ways. It can mean (1) accept as true, (2) credit something with truth, (3) expect or suppose, (4) to have faith, (5) to have confidence in the truth or the existence of something. There are other definitions, other ways of getting at the meaning of belief or to believe, but these give us enough difficulty. If we are to believe what Jesus says, does that mean we accept it fully as truth—or do we just suppose that it might be true? Or are we confident that it is so?

Perhaps we could narrow it down, for our deepest beliefs rule our lives. If our actions suggest one of these definitions, then we need to look at what we do in order to tell ourselves what we believe.

Cayce ventured one perspective: "Study that thou sayest, that thou doest, and reserve *nothing*—in strength of body or mind—in service to others, *that is* a reflection of that He would have thee do, as thou knowest how. As was given by Him, let thine works, thine efforts, be even as was said by Him—'If ye will not believe me, ye *will* believe for the very works' sake—for the things I do bespeak *that* I believe I *am!*' " (262-12)

Another way of saying what we believe is simply by demonstrating what we are doing. The best way to do that? Reserve nothing in our efforts to live the best that we know, in energy, in action, in what we have—as we seek to serve others. This is how to be Christlike, how to become more Godlike. For we are gods in the making.

In another reading, Cayce pointed out that the Water of Life is there for us to drink of freely. He is that Water and that Life. As we simply take hold of ourselves and *do* to others those things that speak of helping, serving, then the blessings come and His promises will be fulfilled.

What you ask in Jesus' name, believing, will be answered in *you, if* your purposes and desires are made wholly one with His will. This is one of the great promises. Believe it.

Do we "suppose" (believe) that this will happen, or do we put our lives in motion to do what we know to do? Some would say that that is what commitment is all about: putting our efforts wholly into action, persistently and patiently, and letting the Creative Energies work through us. It requires a choice, and we might then be under the judgment of "By their fruits ye shall know them." And the results will follow.

> He that receiveth a prophet in the name of a prophet shall receive a prophet's reward. He that makes manifest in self the *will* of the Father, through the application of *that in* hand, and letteth the light so shine that not even the *evil* is spoken good of nor the good spoken evil of, becometh one *with* the Father. 900-465

> Yet the promise has been, "I go to the Father— and greater things ye shall do in my name. For I will bear witness of you—that love me and keep my commandments."

This is the sure way, the pure way—this is the way individuals may so attune their bodies, their minds, their souls, to be healers, to be interpreters, to be ministers, to be the various channels of blessings to others.

These choose thou. As to whether the spirits bear witness with thee—these are to be judged by thine own interpretation of the results obtained. For, as He hath given, "By their fruits ye shall know them." 3019-1

For whosoever will, let him take of the water of life freely. He is that water. He is that life. And as ye take hold and *do*—not merely having the knowledge, but *do* to thy fellow man day by day—so will His blessings, so will His promises, so will His glory, His abilities to work through thee, become manifested.

What saith He? "Greater works than I have done ye may do, for I go to the Father; and as ye abide in me and I in you, so may the glory of the Father be manifested in thy dealings with thy fellow man; that the Father may be glorified in the hearts and the lives, and the children of men." 1809-1

Yet, as is seen in the words of the Master, "Greater works than I do shall *ye* do in my name." That is, wherein and when the entity uses self in that same way and manner in which the Master used self in the material world the entity, through that same force as applied by the Master in the physical world, may do even greater works than seen, for, though they may not be in the manner of walking on the water, or stilling the storm on the sea, yet the compassing of space, and the transmuting of faith, power, force, strength, to the heart of the weary and the heavy laden becomes even greater than these material conditions seen of men, that *their* faith might be made strong in Him. 900-243

John 14:13

Indeed anything you ask in my name I will do, so that the Father may be glorified in the Son. (N.E.B.)

And whatsoever ye shall ask in my name, that will I do, that the Father may be glorified in the Son. (A.V.)

Whatever you ask in my name, I will do it, that the Father may be glorified in the Son ... (C.B.)

... give of thy strength of spirit in making others aware that they, too, may know the Christ as their personal Savior in *every* need, in every hour.

This is done by living that life first in self and then sending it out in His name to those that seek through the aid thou, with others, may be in fulfilling that which is promised by Him, "As ye ask in my name, believing, that will be done in thy experience that the Father may be glorified in me and I in you." 281-20

For all prayer is answered. Don't tell God how to answer it. Make thy wants known to Him. Live as if ye expected them to be answered. For He has given, "What ye ask in my name, believing, that will my Father in heaven give to thee." Again it has been said, and truly, the Father will not withhold any good thing from those who love His coming.

Are ye ever fearful? Are ye ever condemning? The judgment or condemnation with which ye look on others, is that which will be directed to thee. For as ye treat others, so ye treat thy Maker. 4028-1

The law of the Lord is perfect, and it faileth not

when ye allow same to be magnified in thee—thy works, thy thoughts, thy deeds! Then hold to the light that is found in the promises of the Christ, "What ye ask in my name, *believing*—and doing my will—will be answered in *thee*, if thy purposes and thy desires are made wholly one with same." These are thy promises—not just for others! For until ye have known the Lord thy God as *thy* God, personally, ye have only heard of truth! 254-101

Not by what you say but what you are. These are the things that will grow most in the experience of those to whom ye have given and do give spiritual and mental help. For as the entity has found, there has been only the need to express the desire and it has come to pass in thy experience. This is the very nature, the very practice of that He has given; that what ye ask in His name, believing, is done already. Because it doesn't happen today doesn't indicate that it won't happen tomorrow. Because tomorrow never comes, unless today is filled with grace and love. 3954-1

John 14:14

If you ask anything in my name I will do it. (N.E.B.)

If ye shall ask any thing in my name, I will do it. (A.V.)

If you ask anything in my name, I will do it. (C.B.)

Ask in His Name, *Believing*

If you have read these two verses (the thirteenth and fourteenth) and the selections from the Cayce readings, you have these promises about asking explained in a number of ways. If we believe what Jesus was saying, we can ask anything in His name, *believing*—and doing His will—and it will happen. What is His will? To love one another, "just being gentle, just showing forth patience, just showing forth brotherly love as ye add to thyself faith, hope. For in thine faith, in thine hope, in thine patience may it be counted to thee as righteousness. And . . . 'They that keep my words, they that ask shall receive, even that which is the desire of their hearts' that is in keeping with *His* purposes in the experiences of each soul." (688-3)

These bring to us the ability to ask whatever we want, deep in our hearts, and it will be given us. This is true in the mental and the spiritual realms as well as the physical. Many years ago I asked Elsie Sechrist, author of *Dreams—Your Magic Mirror,* what I needed to do to become a better speaker. She said simply that what I am would be more important than anything I might say. The readings state that "Not by what you say but what you are. These are the things that will grow most in the experience of those to whom ye have given and do give spiritual and mental help." (3954-1)

A young lady who is starting a holistic center is wise beyond her years. She is deeply involved in the essence of the Cayce readings. She told me, "I know that everything I ask for will come about because I have seen it happen over and over in my life. I have to be careful what I ask for." She reminded me of the individual for whom the following reading was given: "For as the entity has found, there has been only the need to express the desire and it has come to pass in thy experience. This is the very nature, the very practice of that He has given; that what ye ask in His name, believing, is done already. Because it doesn't happen today doesn't indicate that it won't happen tomorrow. Because tomorrow never comes, unless today is filled with grace and love." (3954-1)

In my own experience, I have found that when I am able to manifest in my relationships with others those qualities we know as the fruits of the Spirit, it brings more peace to my soul and moves me closer to being able to *know* that I can then ask and will be answered with an affirmative.

So, we are gods in the making, if we hold to Him and not to self. We can be joyous in knowing that we each are counted to be worthy to be a channel, an opportunity for someone else to find his or her way. For we were created in His image and are on our way back to claim our rightful heritage. It happens when we *do* that we know to do that may be counted to God for righteousness. The soul growth happens even when we try to do that which we think God wants us to do and fail in the effort. For He loves us and forgives all our mistakes.

> . . . just being gentle, just showing forth patience, just showing forth brotherly love as ye add to thyself faith, hope. For in thine faith, in thine hope, in thine patience may it be counted to thee as righteousness. And they that be in the Lord's service are counted as worthy of *full* acceptations, and to such is given that which may shine forth even as He has promised. "They that keep my words, they that ask shall receive, even that which is the desire of their hearts" that is in keeping with *His* purposes in the experiences of each soul. 688-3

> . . . He is the light and the way; and they that follow in the light may find rest from all those things, those conditions that disturb the soul, the body, the mind.

Let that mind be in thee that was in Him that

promised that "What ye ask in my name, believing, that might ye have in thine experience."

This is applicable in the mental, the spiritual, the material realms. Know they are one, for that ye do unto the mind, unto the body, ye do unto your soul. 378-38

... as has been given, were bodies to hold in their inmost beings a condition desired, and act like they expect to receive it, it would come. That is what is meant, "What is asked in my name that will the Father give unto thee." 900-103

This applies to thee—yea, to each soul, to be sure; but make it thine own cry, *with* the *willingness* in self to be led, to be guided, to be directed, by that as *He* hath given, "Ask in my name and ye—believing—shall have."

Can there be a greater promise? Oft ye, as so many, feel—or act—as if this meant someone else.

Is not thy soul as precious in His sight as though ye had taken a city, yea as though ye had directed a nation?

For ye are gods in thine own making, if ye hold to Him. Not in self, as of self's disappointment. Know that disappointment is with Him, and He is just as hurt. But be ye rather joyous that ye are counted worthy to be a channel, an opportunity, through which even one soul may find the way. For he that hath saved a soul hath indeed covered a multitude of shortcomings! 165-26

John 14:15

If you love me you will obey my commands. (N.E.B.)

If ye love me, keep my commandments. (A.V.)

If you love me, you will keep my commandments. (C.B.)

A Commandment to Love—Very Simple!

We say that God is Love. We were created by Love, by God—this is our belief. What are we to do, then, in following the path of the Master, the Christ, and making Him come alive in our lives? He did not say, "Climb the ladder of success and become the president, or a teacher, a minister, or a ditch-digger"—all honorable professions. But first of all, and the *only* reason we have entered this sphere, is to learn what Jesus meant for us to do when He said, "If you love me, you will keep my commandments."

What are His commandments? Love God and love your fellow man. How is that to be done? Many ways, perhaps, but the heart of it is to do good, to speak gently, to forgive those who treat us in "the darkness of their hearts." To love is to be joyful in the midst of misfortune, to understand and forgive those who do not love us and who treat us with anger and distrust. To love is to accept our mate with all his or her warts and rough spots, and return selfishness with generosity. We *can* love by making ourselves one with the Father, for we are told that we are gods in the making. And we were designed to enjoy that oneness with God.

It doesn't come easy, and it hurts often, but we can choose to be kind, to be patient, to create peace, love, and understanding.

It sounds so simple; yet, like the image of God, it is so difficult to understand. It continues to present us with opportunities to simply love and, as a result, experience soul growth.

In Cayce's words, all these difficult situations are of our own making. We are meeting our own selves and our own undoings. We can tie them up with the "bonds of Love as He gave." (845-1) Then we can throw them away and find life's pathways growing brighter.

For God walks and talks with those that keep His ways. That promise is fulfilled as we love God and keep His commandments. He will come and abide with us. Then it is that we become more aware of the Christ Consciousness "abiding in [us] always." (609-1)

Then Jesus promised to pray to the Father that He would give us another Comforter, the Spirit of Truth, that may abide with us forever. In the Cayce readings it was posed that Jesus said, "I go to the Father, and if I go I will *send* my spirit and he will abide with thee *always,* even unto the end of the earth." (1742-4) It has always been, in humankind's experience, a mystery as to how Jesus' Spirit is within and part of us, but that's the promise.

We are alive through the Spirit of God dwelling within us. Without that Spirit, we are no longer in the Earth. Jesus said that it was not He who did the works that others saw Him do, but rather the Father, who worked in and through Him. We live because God dwells within and gives us life. If the Holy Spirit, the Comforter, is Jesus' Spirit, then it can be considered that the Spirit of God and the Spirit of the Christ both dwell within that temple that is our body.

As we *allow* the Spirit to work within us—that which we can understand is the nature of the Christ and of God—then we are manifesting God in our own lives, in relationship to all those whom we meet, in whatever situation. That is following the commandment to love one another and love God. Simple, isn't it?

But keeping that attitude as pronounced, let thy yeas be yea, thy nays be nay. Follow closely in those purposes that arise in thy daily meditations. For, in judgments of self, that as He has given should ever be that pattern, that measurement by which judgments of self, of others, of conditions, of circumstance is to be drawn: "If ye love me ye will keep my commandments. My commandments are not grievous, but that ye love one another, even as I have loved you." And He thought it not robbery to make self equal with the Father. 585-9

For, as He gave, "If ye love me ye will keep my commandments, ye will take my cross upon thee and learn of me; for my yoke is easy and my burden is light, if ye will bear it in me and not of thyself." For meeting thine own self and thine own undoings will ye bind them with the bonds of love as He gave when He came unto His own and His own received Him not. So as ye come to thine weakness, find thine strength and thine power and thine love in Him; and life's pathways will grow brighter, though the road may be rough, though there may be words that are harsh. Yet as thou lookest upon that tower of strength in thine seal as of the pyramid, as thou reliest upon the cross of Him who bore it for thee, the rose of love, light and radiance will bear thee up, and thou wilt not dash thy foot against a stone. 845-1

. . . God walks and talks with those that keep His ways. "If ye love me, keep my commandments, and I will come and abide with thee," that ye may become more and more aware of that in thine own experience that will bring the awareness of the Christ Consciousness abiding in thee always. 609-1

The line has gone out into that we call space, and

how hast thou looked as to where that line would fall? One with Him, to be guided by Him, or to the aggrandizing of those petty jealousies, those petty hatreds that arise from slights, from slurs in thine daily life. What! Will ye allow self to separate self, the real self, from the living Christ? *He* calls ever, "If ye love me, keep my commandments." What are His commandments? "Love one another." Do good, speak gently, even to those that thou in thine darkness of heart feel would do thee an injustice. 254-68

John 14:16

. . . and I will ask the Father, and he will give you another to be your Advocate, who will be with you for ever . . . (N.E.B.)

And I will pray the Father, and he shall give you another Comforter, that he may abide with you for ever . . . (A.V.)

And I will pray the Father, and he will give you another Counselor, to be with you for ever . . . (C.B.)

For, as was given—"I go away, that I may prepare a place, that where I am there ye may be also. If I go *not* away, the *comforter* will not come"—Did my spirit not bear witness with His Spirit, it would not be possible then for the God within thine self to bear witness with thyself that ye may be brought to the oneness with the Father. 900-335

. . . these should be builded *ever* by the spiritual self; for as the mental body *is* aware of the spiritual aptitudes, or the spiritual movements, so does the promise *become* manifest, that "I go to the father, and if I go I will *send* my spirit and he will abide with thee *always,* even unto the end of the earth." So, as the spirit moves thee, so let thy yeas and thy nays be governed by that, and as the activities must be manifest in the material world, so do they *find expressions through* the material mind, but is the motivative forces *of* that mind of the *Spirit.* The *Spirit is* Truth! 1742-4

John 14:17

The Spirit of Truth. The world cannot receive him, because the world neither sees nor knows him; but you know him, because he dwells with you and is in you. (N.E.B.)

Even the Spirit of truth; whom the world cannot receive, because it seeth him not, neither knoweth him: but ye know him; for he dwelleth with you, and shall be in you. (A.V.)

... even the Spirit of truth, whom the world cannot receive, because it neither sees him nor knows him; you know him, for he dwells with you, and will be in you. (C.B.)

Let not thine good be evil-spoken of. Conduct thy going in and coming out in the manner and way in keeping with that as is being contemplated. Keep thine face toward the light. Trust in thine God, and in the promises of Him who gave: "If thou believest me, keep my commandments, and I will pray the Father, and He will send that Spirit that shall abide with thee, and keep thee when thou goest in and comest out." 254-37

John 14:18

I will not leave you bereft; I am coming back to you. (N.E.B.)

I will not leave you comfortless: I will come to you. (A.V.)

I will not leave you desolate; I will come to you. (C.B.)

. . . He has given, "Lo, I am *with* those who love me even unto the end. I will not leave thee comfortless. I will come to thee," as oft as *thou* within thine self will *let*, will desire, will make self a channel for the expressions of that love which *made* Him the Savior of men. 413-3

The Lord thy God is *one*—as thou art one.

Then, be one—in thy purpose. Know, as given of old, the man called Jesus is the Savior of the world. He has purchased with His own will that right for direction. And He has promised, "I will never leave thee—I will not forsake thee," save that *thou*—as an individual—cast Him out, or reject Him, for counsel from some other source. 2970-1

Let those that have been purposes in thy heart be kept; for though the trials ofttimes overshadow thee, know the strength is not of thyself but as He has given, "I will not leave thee." Ye turn only thy conscience, thy face from Him and feel He hath gone, but His promises are *sure*—and He is able to keep them! Turn thou to Him! 254-95

Then, in applying self, my son, know that the Father liveth in thee, and will rightly guide thee in thy seeking and in thine steps day by day, if thou hast prepared His temple in thee for the place that He may abide. If thou keepest the temple cluttered up with those things that bespeak rather of the flesh, only the flesh can answer—but if thou keepest the temple clean and decorated in the spirit of love, and in the light of truth, then it will shed its light abroad, even as He has given, "I will not leave thee comfortless but will come and abide with thee, that ye may be my children and I will be your god." 440-4

John 14:19

In a little while the world will see me no longer, but you will see me; because I live, you too will live ... (N.E.B.)

Yet a little while, and the world seeth me no more; but ye see me: because I live, ye shall live also. (A.V.)

Yet a little while, and the world will see me no more, but you will see me; because I live, you will live also. (C.B.)

Be sure that everything is done in decency and order, and there is not the attempt to measure spiritual things by material standards, nor *material* things by *spiritual* standards; for each to their own place. All are not to be prophets, nor all readers, nor all ministers, but each according to that as has been given through the ministry of each individual's self in their various phases and spheres of development. Let that mind be in each as was in Him, that "if ye believe in me, greater things than I have done *ye shall do!* for I go to the Father, and as ye live in me ye may live in the Father also." 254-60

John 14:20

... then you will know that I am in my Father, and you in me and I in you. (N.E.B.)

At that day ye shall know that I am in my Father, and ye in me, and I in you. (A.V.)

In that day you will know that I am in my Father, and you in me, and I in you. (C.B.)

Then in thy dealings (and remain in same) sow the seeds of friendships, of love, of patience, of long-suffering, of kindness, of grace; and ye will find more and more that life and its dealings with others become worthwhile—beauty and the joy of living becomes part of the experience. And more and more will the love be poured out to thee, for His promises are sure—that as ye sow the seeds of righteousness, the seeds of the spirit of truth, "I and the Father will come and make our abode with thee— to do thee good."

... Do ye entertain Him, do ye make for Him an abode? Or does He stand only and knock? And it is not the knowledge of Him but the knowledge *in* Him that counts. For as ye live and move and have thy being in the Father, so in Him is the manner, the way of life itself. 1765-2

What is karma but giving way to impulse? Just as has been experienced by this entity, when the entity has sung Halleluiah it was much harder to say "dammit."

Hence we find that, even under stress, He goeth

with thee—*all* the way. For as He has given, "If ye will but ask, I will *come*—I will *abide*—I will be with thee!"

Thus may the entity use its abilities, its talents, its voice. For, know that all thy attributes and activities of the senses are the gifts of God. This is true with every entity, but especially with this entity. For he that sings, he that sees, he that speaks, he that hears well is especially *gifted* of God; and not only has the one or the two but the five talents that may be made into such measures—by the choice of the entity—that he may be ruler not only over the five senses but the ten kingdoms in God's own way! 622-6

Oft ye may ask, from thy enquiring mind, when I so desire to know Him, why then do I not see, do I not hear?

How long, O Lord, how long? Look not for a sign, as a *sign*, as He gave, but *be*—and ye *are* as one with Him!

These become not as trites, not as sayings—they must be *experienced* by self! They may not be experienced by merely being told. Ye live them! "As ye live in me and I in the Father, ask what ye will and it will be done unto thee."

Ye wait, then, knowing. He knoweth what thou hast need of before ye ask. Then ye say, Why ask?

In the love of thine children, is it those who ask or those who do not ask that make a response? Not that ye love one more than the other; not for impunity, but a reciprocal reaction!

Those things are as God is. And they that would know Him must *believe* that He is; and most of all *act* that way! 1158-9

... "If ye will be mine, then I in you and I in the Father," ye may know that as may bring to the experiences of many the greater knowledge, the greater interpretation of life, its purposes in the earth, those activities for the relationships of God to man, man's relationship to his fellow man. These should be as one.

For that as we find in our fellow man is a reflection of that we think of our Creative Forces. 1226-1

John 14:21

The man who has received my commands and obeys them—he it is who loves me; and he who loves me will be loved by my Father; and I will love him and disclose myself to him. (N.E.B.)

He that hath my commandments, and keepeth them, he it is that loveth me; and he that loveth me shall be loved of my Father, and I will love him, and will manifest myself to him. (A.V.)

He who has my commandments and keeps them, he it is who loves me; and he who loves me will be loved by my Father, and I will love him and manifest myself to him. (C.B.)

To Be Obedient Is to Experience True Life

Obedience to the laws of the earth certainly keeps us out of trouble. Obedience to the suggestions of a friend who is outside the law, for instance, is to court disaster. Obedience to light keeps us from stumbling. Darkness clouds our vision and may lead us astray.

When my children were small, I told them before our trips that while we were traveling in our VW bus, they

were to obey me completely when I gave them an order—like, "Be quiet!" There was always a good reason for
my commands. I could not tell them at the time why,
because the situation might require immediate action
for safety for all of us. Afterward, then, I would explain
why I ordered them in the way that I did. It was for their
good, and I hope they always remembered that. Their
gain was a safe trip.

Jesus gave several commands in these four chapters
of the Gospel of John. Those who obeyed them gained
much in their soul's journey through life. Obedience,
then, is very important—and it is beneficial to remember that one always chooses to whom one will give one's
obedience—whom one chooses to serve. If someone is
going to be a servant, who is that person's boss? With my
children, while I am driving the bus on a trip, I am the boss.
I love my kids, and I want to keep them safe from harm.

In the large picture, when children have grown, even
when I may have become a bit more wise in my actions,
I find we are all on an adventure, seeking the purposes
for which we came into being. My soul recognizes that
Jesus is the Guide whom I choose to follow, and I will
obey to the best of my ability the laws which He set forth.
Remember, He said these words were not His but were
those of the Father who was doing His work in and
through Him.

So, if you or I, or my children, or any of the souls on
the earth are to be obedient to Jesus' commands, what
can we expect? " . . . he it is who loves me; and he who
loves me will be loved by my Father; and I will love him
and disclose myself to him." (John 14:21) Quite a promise—to have Jesus disclose Himself to us! But there is still
that quality of choice which belongs to every man and
woman on this globe and which, in reality, links him or
her to God because we were created in His image. Thus,
we must make those choices, one way or the other.

Jesus commanded us to love God and to love one another. Each of us has our being through God and has the Spirit flowing through us. The Christ is there, too, often totally unrecognized. We are challenged to see the Father in the person we meet, moment by moment. As we love that person, we will in turn be loved by the Father. That is one of the promises. It is part of the Law of the Spirit.

One of the Cayce readings tells us that "In thy daily walks let His light so shine in thine own self that those ye contact may know that the love of the Father is being shown in thy daily conversation, thy daily activities. For, as He gave, he that would show forth the love of the Father will keep His ways day by day. " (262-47) Cayce goes on to tell us that we had best not let those things of the earth that would trouble us interfere with our manifesting love, for the end result, if we keep things clear, will then be that He will come and abide with us, and we shall know Him as He is.

But suppose we don't quite understand what love is when it is offered to another or when it is applied in action toward another. To know love as love in action, in following His commandments, is "just being kind, just being patient, just being long-suffering with thy problems, thy turmoils, thy strifes." (5749-13) Each of us may do this—manifesting the fruits of the Spirit as we move through the earth on our journey.

Cayce repeated this concept in a variety of ways. He said in another reading that "the love as was shown, as was manifested by Him, is *alone* the way, the manner in and through which the soul may become aware of its activity even in a sin-sick world.

"For just being kind, just being gentle, is the means and the manner, the way. Not in a passive way, but even as He—who went about doing *good* each day." (853-9)

There are laws, there are rules for everything. What are

the rules, then? Simply stated, are they not just the living of the fruits of the Spirit? Cayce said, "Ye may become aware of His presence abiding with thee. When ye manifest love, patience, hope, charity, tolerance, faith; these be the manners. Not in thine own *self!* These as words, these as expressions, these as visualized *objects* may be within thine self. But when ye as a soul, as an entity, as an individual, make such manifest to those ye meet casually, to those that ye contact day by day—in conversation, in example, in precept; these the attributes of the Spirit—ye become aware of that Consciousness, of that Christ Spirit, of that Christ Consciousness as He gave, 'Ye abiding in me and I in the Father, *we*—the Father, I will c*ome* and abide with thee.' " (272-9)

This is the promise, then, isn't it? We can accept or reject it, either in part or entirely, but as Mr. Cayce pointed out, "This then is the *greatest* opportunity, the greatest experience!" (1497-2) And why? " . . . all ye ask shall be done, and I will bring to your remembrance *all* things, from the foundations of the world! For ye were indeed with me from the beginning." (1992-1)

> In thy daily walks let His light so shine in thine own self that those ye contact may know that the love of the Father is being shown in thy daily conversation, thy daily activities. For, as He gave, he that would show forth the love of the Father will keep His ways day by day. For, glorying in self is as the activities of self-exaltation, but glorying in the Father, in the Son, is showing forth that He bids thee do day by day. What, then, are His biddings? "Love the Lord thy God with all thine heart, thine soul, and thy neighbor as thyself!" 262-47

> Let thine mind, thine heart and thine purposes be as upon the altar of love to Him whom ye would

serve, thy Master, thy God. For He is mindful ever of those that seek to know His ways; for His ways are not past finding out. For to those that have put on Christ, who have named the Name of Him that promised, "If ye love me, keep my commandments, and I will come and abide with thee; my yoke is easy, my burden is *light* to *those* that *love* the Lord." Let not those things that would trouble thee interfere; for yet a little while and thou should see face to face—even as thou hast been called unto a service to thy fellow man, even as He; for He will not leave thee comfortless, but will come and abide with thee, and thou shalt *know* Him as He is. 262-72

In self may there be manifested that love, even as He showed in thee, in the experiences in the ministering with and for Him; and the promises that were made thee *are* true, if self will be kept in that way in which that spirit of love, of faith, of hope, of charity, may be kept in His way. "If ye love me, keep my commandments" is ever the call of Him. 262-46

John 14:22

Judas asked him—the other Judas, not Iscariot— Lord, what can have happened, that you mean to disclose yourself to us alone and not to the world? (N.E.B.)

Judas saith unto him, not Iscariot, Lord, how is it that thou wilt manifest thyself unto us, and not unto the world? (A.V.)

Judas (not Iscariot) said to him, Lord, how is it that you will manifest yourself to us, and not to the world? (C.B.)

Then, let not your heart be troubled; ye believe in God—believe in Him, who has promised that "If ye will love me and keep my commandments, I will come and abide with thee—for, Lo, I am with thee always."

His commandments are not grievous; just being kind, just being patient, just being long-suffering with thy problems, thy turmoils, thy strifes.

Through that ability to make Himself one with the Father, He has gained that right, that honor to declare Himself unto as many as will harken.

Let thy light, then, shine ever in the dark, in the light; in the sorrow, in the gladness of thy purpose, of thy desire; that He may be glorified even as He asks of the Father.

Ye—each of ye, as individuals—may do this. So ye, as ye come into His presence, may be given "Well done, thou good and faithful brother—enter into the joy of thy Lord." 5749-13

John 14:23

Jesus replied, Anyone who loves me will heed what I say; then my Father will love him, and we will come to him and make our dwelling with him . . . (N.E.B.)

Jesus answered and said unto him, If a man love me, he will keep my words: and my Father will love him, and we will come unto him, and make our abode with him. (A.V.)

Jesus answered him, If a man love me, he will keep my word, and my Father will love him, and we will come to him and make our home with him. (C.B.)

Then with that consciousness of His awareness,
we may know even as He has given, "Ye abide in me,
as I in the Father—I will come and abide with thee."

In that consciousness, then, the purposes for
which each soul enters materiality are that it may
become aware of its relationships to the Creative
Forces or God; by the material manifestation of the
things thought, said, *done,* in relation to its fellow
man! 1567-2

For in a s*piritual* ideal one may conquer the
earth, the mental world, the masses even; but one
that sets its ideal in an individual, or that which is
of the earth-earthy, may be finding self stumbling
over that it has set as its idea or ideal. For, as He has
given, "If ye will abide in that I have given thee, I
will come and abide with thee and give thee that
necessary for not only thine speech but thine activity, thine purpose, thine desire in the earth." For if
we would attain to that which is of the soul, for its
own development, we will follow in those precepts
that *He,* thine Savior, thine Ideal, has set before
thee! 361-4

What are the rules, then? As has just been out-
lined, ye may become aware of His presence abiding with thee. When ye manifest love, patience,
hope, charity, tolerance, faith; these be the manners. Not in thine own *self!* These as words, these as
expressions, these as visualized *objects* may be
within thine self. But when ye as a soul, as an entity,
as an individual, make such manifest to those ye
meet casually, to those that ye contact day by day—
in conversation, in example, in precept; these the
attributes of the Spirit—ye become aware of that
Consciousness, of that Christ Spirit, of that Christ

Consciousness as He gave, "Ye abiding in me and I in the Father, *we*—the Father, I will *come* and abide with thee."

When the Spirit of the Father, when the activities that the Christ—the man—gave to the sons of men—are made manifest in thine own life day by day, then ye become aware of His presence abiding in thee. 272-9

But the opportunities are as great today. For ye in the present have the knowledge that He lived, that He not only lived but that He *lives*—and is mindful of those that seek to honor the Father! that He will come and abide—with the Father—with those who seek to do the Father's biddings.

This is a promise. Ye have the opportunities to either accept or reject same, wholeheartedly or in part; or to be seen of men or to satisfy or *justify* self before thine own conscience or before the thought of thy fellow man!

This then is the *greatest* opportunity, the greatest experience! 1497-2

John 14:24

... but he who does not love me does not heed what I say. And the word you hear is not mine: it is the word of the Father who sent me. (N.E.B.)

He that loveth me not keepeth not my sayings: and the word which ye hear is not mine, but the Father's which sent me. (A.V.)

He who does not love me does not keep my words; and the word which you hear is not mine but the Father's who sent me. (C.B.)

. . . be not confused. Love Him. For He hath promised, "If ye abide in me, as I abide in the Father, I will come and abide with thee; and all ye ask shall be done, and I will bring to your remembrance *all* things, from the foundations of the world! For ye were indeed with me from the beginning."

He *alone*—as ye understand and know—is able to keep that He hath promised thee. 1992-1

John 14:25

I have told you all this while I am still here with you . . . (N.E.B.)

These things have I spoken unto you, being yet present with you. (A.V.)

These things I have spoken to you, while I am still with you. (C.B.)

. . . "In my Father's house are many mansions; were it not so I would have told you. I go to prepare a place, that where I am ye may be also. Me ye have known, and the way ye know, for I am the way, the truth, and the light. Had ye not known me ye would not have known the Father, but seeing me, in me ye see the Father also. If I go not away the spirit will not come unto you, but I go to the Father, and the spirit will *abide* with you and bring to your *remembrance* all things whatsoever I have said unto you." These—this, mine son—and thou wilt see, even in the counsel of thine own hearts, as men, *this* fulfilled in the street, in the market place, or in thine *own* home. 137-123

John 14:26

... but your Advocate, the Holy Spirit whom the
Father will send in my name, will teach you every-
thing, and will call to mind all that I have told you.
(N.E.B.)

But the Comforter, which is the Holy Ghost, whom
the Father will send in my name, he shall teach you
all things, and bring all things to your remembrance, whatsoever I have said unto you. (A.V.)

But the Counselor, the Holy Spirit, whom the Father will send in my name, he will teach you all
things, and bring to your remembrance all that I
have said to you. (C.B.)

Study not with what *others* have said, but with
what thou hast found in thine own experience of
what John has given as respecting His words, of
what Mark has given as to His deeds, His acts; for in
Him is the light. "Understandest thou that I will
bring to remembrance those things that will give
thee the answer to the questions that arise in thy
experience in all of thine undertakings for me?"

So, as in that day when conviction came in thine
experience, reason not *out* of same; rather listen to
the Voice that arises, that—even as He gave, "Flesh
and blood revealed this not to thee, but my Father
in heaven"—has given thee the power to be the
minister of Me to many. 452-6

... "He that takes my yoke upon him and learns
of me, with *him* will I abide day by day, and all
things will be brought to remembrance that I have
given thee since the foundations of the world, for

thou were with me in the beginning and thou may abide with me in that day when the earth will be rolled as the scroll; for the heavens and the earth will pass away, but my word shall *not* pass away." The promises in Him are sure—the way ye know! 262-28

. . . know—as ye apply, as ye ask, as ye manifest, as ye recall—more and more is recalled to thee. This is memory. For, know the basic principle comes in Him as He has given, "I will bring *all* things to thy memory from the foundation of the world."

Do not think, then, that the mind of any active individual may ever be such as to be overburdened with memories, but make them ever a helpful influence.

To be sure, many individuals have set rules as to how courses in memory are set by associations. But most of these, or many, have been only for material gains.

Thy life is not set as one for purely the material things. For, know, the earth and all therein is the Lord's. The silver, the gold, the cattle on a thousand hills are His. He knows thy needs, but thou must *choose* as to what ye will do with the talents He hath given thee.

As ye apply, as ye make use of that in hand, more is given thee. For, day unto day is sufficient, if use is made thereof; not to self, not to self alone. Not that self is not to be considered, but losing self in good is the better way to *find* self.

What is good? How is such defined in thy life—of awakening to all the possibilities that exist in thy intake of life and its phases? To do good is to think constructively, to think creatively. What is creative, what is constructive, ye may ask? That which never hinders, which never makes for the bringing of any harm to others. 1206-13

For His promises have been to bring to the re-membrance of those who love Him the knowledge that needs be for the souls to manifest in the mate-rial plane that needed for not only their *own* devel-opment but for the very joy and hope and life for the others that such will aid in their activities through this material experience.

Think not more highly of thyself than ye ought to think. For He humbled Himself and became as one with the lowest of men—that love might be made manifest. So may ye, in the humbleness of heart, come to know the greater glory by and through the greater service ye may render to thy fellow man.

Harmonize thy life as ye do the tones of nature itself; and more joy and beauty will be in thy daily experience. 262-121

John 14:27

Peace is my parting gift to you, my own peace, such as the world cannot give. Set your troubled hearts at rest, and banish your fears. (N.E.B.)

Peace I leave with you, my peace I give unto you; not as the world giveth, give I unto you. Let not your heart be troubled, neither let it be afraid. (A.V.)

Peace I leave with you; my peace I give to you; not as the world gives do I give to you. Let not your hearts be troubled, neither let them be afraid. (C.B.)

Add unto thy faith works, that showeth forth those attributes that are expressions of His Spirit in the world. So shall it, the faith, become the evidence of things not seen, and His grace, His mercies, will abide with you whithersoever thou goest. Peace be with thee! Not as the world gives peace; rather as that that has lost self, self's personality, in Him. 262-15

Not as the world knoweth peace, but that conviction within the heart, that though the experiences of the physical are oft as torments in our material experience, there is the advocate with the Father and He will comfort, He will bring peace, harmony and understanding to those who seek to know His face—and who have the courage to dare to do the right in the face of all oppositions of every nature. The unkindnesses, the slights, the slurs, the unkind words, the broken promises of men become as naught in the praise of Him who gave His life that we might have life more abundantly in Him, and gives the promise that through the prayer, through the desire, through the trying to be that as we know, as we feel is in keeping with the promises in the Christ they become (the promises) then our very own.

Then in so living and so realizing may we each become as channels of blessings to others in their disturbed minds, their disturbed bodies, their disturbed desires. For if we would be one with Him, it is in helping others, in bringing to them the knowledge of the Christ, that His peace—which is of Him—becomes a part of us.

For if we would have life, we must give life—that we may have it more abundantly. For life is the manifestation of the Father in the earth. 281-35

For only the spiritual forces for thine soul endure forever. And those lessons that each individual learns by its disappointments, fears, sorrows, are not as tiers that make for a weakening but rather as tiers that may be builded up to climb to greater heights, and greater understandings—if they will but be put or brought into those forces where—in the temple of self—where the own God may give the individual peace. Not as the world giveth peace but as only the knowledge that thy soul, thy inner self is in accord and at-oneness with Him. 1183-1

Yet so clothe self with the beauties of those things expressed in nature, those things expressed in the more uplifting moments of individual activity, as to keep that peace, that balance, that makes for the realization that even though there be not fame or even fortune, those that *love* the Lord, that keep His ways, find that peace which passeth understanding. Not as the world gives peace but rather as the Prince of Peace gave, "Ye that abide in me shall *know* the truth and the truth shall indeed make ye *free*" from those turmoils, those strifes that make men afraid. 1157-1

John 14:28

You heard me say, "I am going away, and coming back to you." If you loved me you would have been glad to hear that I was going to the Father; for the Father is greater than I. (N.E.B.)

Ye have heard how I said unto you, I go away, and come again unto you. If ye loved me, ye would rejoice, because I said, I go unto the Father: for my Father is greater than I. (A.V.)

You heard me say to you, I go away, and I will come to you. If you loved me, you would have rejoiced, because I go to the Father; for the Father is greater than I. (C.B.)

Then gather together, even as He gave; "Let not your hearts be troubled; ye believe in God, believe also in me. And I go to the Father, and if ye love me ye will keep my commandments. For my commandments are not grievous, but are *living* and *doing* day by day those things that ye *know* to do!"

Patience, love, gentleness! Not gainsaying, not finding fault!

These be the little things, yet bespeak that fact that ye have known, ye do know, and ye entertain the Spirit of the Christ!

If ye do these, then, there is no question as to whether "I shall do this or that," for the Spirit of the Christ will and does direct thee! If ye live the Christ life! 262-117

How have the promises read that the Son has given? "I go to prepare a place that where I am there ye may be also. I will come again and receive you unto myself." Then, as the individual heart attunes its mind and its body-activity into that consciousness of the desire for the hastening of that day. Yet the merciful kindness of the Father has, in the eyes of many, delayed the coming, and many have cried even as the parable He gave, "We know not what has become of this man. Show us other gods that may lead us in this day." Yet the cry in the heart and the soul of those that seek His way is to hasten that day. Yet, as He has given, in patience, in listening, in being still, may ye know that the Lord doeth all things well. Be not weary that He apparently prolongs His

time, for—as the Master has given, "As to the day,
no man knoweth, not even the son, but the Father
and they to whom the Father may reveal the Son
prepareth the way that all men may know the love
of the Father." And as ye would be the channel to
hasten that glorious day of the coming of the Lord,
then do with a might that thy hands find to do to
make for the greater manifestations of the love of
the Father in the earth. 262-58

John 14:29

**I have told you now, beforehand, so that when it
happens you may have faith. (N.E.B.)**

**And now I have told you before it come to pass,
that, when it is come to pass, ye might believe.
(A.V.)**

**And now I have told you before it takes place, so
that when it does take place, you may believe.
(C.B.)**

And, as He has given, "A new commandment give
I unto you, that ye love one another," that ye keep
that which is committed unto thee against that day
when each must in its own way present that it has
builded in its experience as a service unto Him that
gave, "If ye love me, keep my commandments, and
I will come and abide with thee. I will not leave thee
comfortless, but will give that ye ask in my name,
believing, for I go to the Father and ye that abide in
me abide in the Father also."
    ... He that is called into service does show forth
in the life day by day that he has walked close with
Him. For, while shadows, doubts and fears arise, the

promises are sure that if the fruits of the spirit are shown in thy life the harvest will be the Lord's increase in thine experience. 473-1

John 14:30-31

I shall not talk much longer with you, for the Prince of this world approaches. He has no rights over me; but the world must be shown that I love the Father, and do exactly as he commands; so up, let us go forward. (N.E.B.)

Hereafter I will not talk much with you: for the prince of this world cometh, and hath nothing in me. But that the world may know that I love the Father; and as the Father gave me commandment, even so I do. Arise, let us go hence. (A.V.)

I will no longer talk much with you, for the ruler of this world is coming. He has no power over me; but I do as the Father has commanded me, so that the world may know that I love the Father. Rise, let us go hence. (C.B.)

How Do We Learn Obedience?

In the last part of the fourteenth chapter, Jesus told His disciples that "the Prince of this world approaches. He has no rights over me; but the world must be shown that I love the Father, and do exactly as he commands; so up, let us go forward." (v. 30-31) There is something very important about obedience. We either obey those in command or we reject them.

Sometimes we hear as commands what is said as instruction. But we don't want to hear *commands,* so we develop hearing problems.

It's difficult to comprehend why God, the Creator, the God Force, the Power of Love that brought all things into being, would command Jesus to move through this incarnation in perfect agreement with His will, and then end His life on the cross. Perhaps we can come closer to an understanding when we remember that our destiny is to be a companion with God, to experience a oneness with Him—to be a cocreator with Him.

Jesus was, at this point, in the process of fulfilling this oneness through obedience to the Highest Power, allowing no influence from the Prince of this World to affect Him. It was through this One we know as Jesus, the Word, the Light of Men, that all things in the earth came into being in the beginning (John 1:1-4). While He was without what we know as sin, death on the cross symbolized His overcoming the earth, which He, in the first place, created. The overcoming made it possible that we might have a Way to that same oneness with God.

It's a mystical concept, as is the earth itself mystical, harboring within its life the law of cause and effect. There are, in reality, no karmic debts from this or other sojourns that cannot be set aside in "Lord, have Thy ways with me." The Way, of course, is the Way of Love, for we have said, over the centuries, that God *is* Love. Cayce seemed to see this in so many different situations. To a thirty-eight-year-old man who wanted to know where he would be incarnated next time and with whom, the reading had this to say:

> Better get into shape so that you can incarnate. That depends a great deal upon what one does about the present opportunities. It isn't set for time immemorial as to be what you will be from one experience to the other. For, as has been given, there are unchangeable laws. The Creator intended man to be a companion with Him. Whether in heaven or

in the earth or in whatever consciousness, a companion with the Creator. How many will it require for thee to be able to be a companion with the Creative Forces wherever you are? That is also a law. What ye sow, ye reap. What is, then, that which is making for the closer association of body, mind, and soul to Father, Son and Holy Spirit? Just as has been indicated in thy physical being—there are those tendencies for auditory disturbances. Ye have heard. Have ye heeded?

In those, then, to be the applications, what becomes disturbing? He that heeds not, then, has rejected, and there is the need for remembering the unchangeable law: "Though He were the Son, yet learned He obedience through the things which He suffered." Shall thou be greater than thy Lord? Where will these occur? Where do you make them? The place where you art, is the place to begin. What were the admonitions? "Use that thou hast in hand. Today, will ye hear His voice, harden not thy heart." 416-18

In other words, we need to listen, to be willing to obey what we gain from the voice within our own body, our temple. As we listen, as we make our loving response active in our lives in relation to others, then we come to experience the Spirit dwelling within our bodies, and the promise will begin to unfold that: " ' . . . all things will be brought to remembrance that I have given thee since the foundations of the world, for thou were with me in the beginning and thou may abide with me in that day when the earth will be rolled as the scroll; for the heavens and the earth will pass away, but my word shall *not* pass away.' The promises in Him are sure—the way ye know!" (262-28)

Jesus promised us that His way is not hard. So, must

we suffer or not? It seems that suffering only comes about when we reject, when we say, "I want my way!" Suffering comes when we are still in rebellion—when we want to get even with others, when we hate those who do not treat us right, when things that are "mine" are taken from me, when we blame the world for mistreating us. We may be humbled by forgiving those who take advantage of us, but it creates peace rather than warfare. And the Comforter, the Holy Spirit, has been active then in our lives, and the pain, the hurt is let go of in forgiveness, understanding, and love. There are those two principles, two conflicting forces in the earth today: the prince of this world and that principle that says to every soul, "Fear not, I have overcome the world and the prince of the world hath nothing in me."

Cayce said it once like this: " . . . though the experiences of the physical are oft as torments in our material experience, there is the advocate with the Father and He will comfort, He will bring peace, harmony and understanding to those who seek to know His face—and who have the courage to dare to do the right in the face of all oppositions of every nature." (281-35)

It's a promise to each one of us! Those commandments that Jesus gave are not difficult—simply living and doing day by day those things that you know to do, that are in accord with "A new commandment give I unto you, that ye love one another."

How, then, do we love that we might manifest the abiding Spirit that always dwells within? First, then, "hold not malice, hold not any of those things in thy mind or purpose that maketh man afraid. For the fruits of the spirit ye know: Patience, love, justice, long-suffering. Against such there is no law. For it is the heart of God that abideth ever, and they know no fear. For it is the love of Him that casteth out fear. And it is that which first came into being—*light*—that may abide ever." (3188-1)

That's how we love, allowing the power of the God-Force and the Light to manifest in all of our dealings with others and with ourselves.

So, then, we ask again, "How do we learn obedience?" The best answer most probably is—practice, practice, practice! Even when it is most difficult, practice obedience—*do it!*

For, He so loved the world as to give His Son. Ye have loved, ye do so love thy fellow man as to give thy mind, thy body, in counsel, in instruction, in those activities that enable the individual souls to think better of themselves and the reason thereof. For, they must learn to live with themselves, even as did He, and to know—though the prince of this world may come, may tempt, may even declare the joy of self-elation—he has no part in them. 2629-1

Know, as He hath indicated in His life, that if there is the determination, the desire to do good, then disturbances as of the world arise. But in thy choice of manner and means of activity, of service, let it be even as He gave, "The prince of this world cometh, but he has no part in me."

So live, so think, so do, that fear, doubt, disturbance of any nature may be wholly cast out; through the trust, the faith, the hope in Him. 1152-13

Just as have been those principles of your present conflict, "Send help, for man's heritage of freedom would be taken away." By whom? He that hath said, "Surely ye will not die." There are those two principles , two conflicting forces in the earth today: the prince of this world, and that principle that says to every soul, "Fear not, I have overcome the world and the prince of the world hath nothing in me."

Can ye say that? Ye must! That is thy hope; that "The prince of this world, Satan, that old serpent, hath no part in any desire of my mind, my heart, my body, that I do not control in the direction it shall take." These are the things, these are the principles. 3976-29

For that desire to procreate in self, or to hold to selfish interests, has grown—grown—until it *is* what did He give?—the prince of this world; the prince of this world!

Know that He who came as our director, as our brother, as our Savior, has said that the prince of this world has no part in Him nor with Him.

Then as we become more and more aware within ourselves of the answering of the experiences, we become aware of what He gave to those that were the first of *God's* projection—not man's but God's projection—into the earth; Adam and Eve.

And then in their early day they were tempted by the prince of this world, and partook of same.

When we see that in ourselves, yes in our own sons, in our own daughters, in our own brothers, in our own husbands, in our own wives, we begin to see how, why that patience becomes a part of that which is the awareness in man of God's presence in the earth.

And we see the ways and means through which such activities were presented to those children that were bestowed with the very power of God, yet not aware of right and wrong. For they were *in* a world ruled by the prince of selfishness, darkness, hate, malice, jealousy, backbiting, uncomely things; not of the beauties, but that self might be taking advantage in this or that way or manner.

What moves the spirit of these activities? *God,*

but—will and choice misdirected.

And these then show the mercy and the patience that He gives forth to each soul in this speck, this dot in the universe. Yet He would have each soul, each one of us, to become even as He—even as He prayed: "Father, may they be with me where I am; that they may behold the glory I had with thee before the foundations of the world."

What do these words mean to us? That the Spirit has quickened us, so that we seek to manifest what? His mercy, His grace, His patience among our fellow men. 262-115

Then as thy body, thy mind, and thy soul are but the three-dimensional phases of thy concept of the Godhead, use each as such. Thy body, indeed, then is the temple of the living God. *There* creation is manifested. Each morning is but another opportunity. The night cometh when no man worketh. What meaneth this? No thought, no purpose, but that the physical resteth. So did He rest on the seventh day. "Take thy rest," saith the Master. "Sleep on and take thy rest—for he cometh. Arise, let's be going for the prince of this world cometh, but he hath no part in me."

So live, day by day, that ye can truly say, then, to self, that ye entertain not in word, in thought or deed the prince of the world; but rather that ye walk oft, daily, with Him, who hath overcome and saith to thee, "Fear not! Indeed offences come, but woe unto them by whom they come." Let that not be said, then, of thee in thy own consciousness. For, trusting in Him, He has said, "Fear not—it is I. I have overcome the world."

So may ye as ye abide in Him; not weekly, hourly, but eternally. 3188-1

3

The Gospel of John, Chapter 15

"I am the real vine, and my Father is the gardener." (John 15:1)

How often do we hear a simile—a figure of speech—and dismiss it with just a cursory moment of time, giving it only superficial attention? In Hampton Court in England, not far from London, there is an awe-inspiring grapevine that has been producing thousands of pounds of grapes yearly for more than two centuries. I have wondered what the gardener had in mind when he planted a wee, small grapevine hundreds of years ago. To think that a vine that perhaps measured only the thickness of a child's little finger would one day be more than three feet in diameter. I've felt a reverence for what the grapevine represents ever since seeing that magnificent creation.

In the countryside where Jesus spent most of His life, and where He told His disciples, "I am the real vine, and my Father is the gardener," there may have been grape-vines like the one at Hampton Court. Those who lived in those areas knew the nature of the grapevine and how the fruit depends on the strength and vigor of the vine for its life and vitality and worthiness.

So this simile might be called a parable that reminds us that all of life—all that we are—depends on our connection to the Source of all life. Both in the Bible and in the Cayce readings, the Source is the power we know as God—eternal beyond our earthly consciousness to understand.

Jesus, recognizing His oneness with God, used the vine and the branches to let us know that we, too, are part of that divine plan and need to be aware of it and act in accordance with what we are. God, as the Gardener, sets the limits and the laws of love and has ultimate power to shape us.

We are an expression of that power, for all of our thoughts, our activities, our very life itself is the manifestation of that original power. When we do good, it is God moving through us doing His good. When we do "bad" or "evil," it is that same Force, distorted and changed to suit our selfish will and our own purposes (at times far removed from God's desires). In a sense, then, in that instance, we are removed from the Source by our own choices, which have developed into patterns and habits in our unconscious minds. Or we might just be constricting the flow of real life within our beings, not truly being removed.

This may be just another way of telling us that we need always to remember where our life and our power originate.

When we take the perspective that is given us in these

readings and in the Bible, we will always experience life in a different way. For we are given the awareness that we were in existence before the worlds came into being, created by God, and destined to still be in existence when the worlds are gone. Our real life is a vibrational reality, not of the earth substance, but formed in such a way here as manifested energy, that we can experience the earthly dimension and find our way, like the prodigal son, back to the Father, who has always loved us and has never turned His back on us.

All of us influence those around us in ways that are sometimes discovered only years hence. Cayce told one young lady that "As the entity is in that position of being an influence, know the source of thy power, thy might. And let the guiding influence in spirit, in truth, be in the individual activities that may bring those powers that are as manifestations in Him who is the way, the truth, the light." (2594-1)

In this fifteenth chapter, much is told us—as if to emphasize what has already been given—of the promises, of what it means to abide in the Christ and in the Father, of His commandments to love one another, of the Comforter, and of the troubles and turmoils that will be experienced by those who follow the light of the Christ.

The Cayce readings that were originally chosen to accompany the different verses should be read carefully and thoughtfully, for they continue to offer us a deeper insight into our own nature and the nature of the Forces that have brought us into being. For instance, the cross was discussed in the previous chapter, but the following reading gives us a better insight into the promises that go with the bearing of one's cross:

"Be of good cheer, for I will stand in the stead of him who puts his trust in me, hath said the Lord, and He is able, and willing, and anxious to do that for those who *love* the coming of the consciousness of self's being emerged [in], ruled, controlled, by His Spirit. Keep that thou hast kept in thine heart, and make this *manifest* in the life.

"In the actions of the body, mental and physical, will come the consciousness of this indwelling sufficient to take away those conditions that have been as those crosses that all must bear in some form, that they too may know that God is in His holy temple and is approached through His Son, who gave to man the *divine* access to that throne room, in that He—as man—suffered in the body, and in the self being lost in service gave *Himself* in that manner the ransom for those that would come, in meekness of heart, knowing that that asked for in His name is done already, even as the heart of self is in accord with that asked *for* for self *in* others. Unto others, then, in the action comes the consciousness of *that* as is gained through belief in His name. Keep constant, then, in prayer, in supplication, and in believing, and acting as if that sought is done already." (1377-1) For it is!

Most of you reading this book understand that we have been in this earth dimension over and over, many times throughout our existence. We know our Source— or, at least, we *should* know our Source. We know about the turmoils and persecutions that abound in the world and in our own lives; we are aware, certainly, that we need to love one another and of the need to follow the path that leads us to our destination.

Cayce gave a reading for a young man who had spent a lifetime in the days of the Master. It speaks to all of us:

Know from whence ye came and whither ye go. For if ye become as anxious about using thyself for the purpose for which ye entered, ye will not be so anxious about where you are going. For remember, it is only self ye are meeting that causes anxieties or any character of trouble. For thou hast been from the beginning. It is up to thee as to whether ye continue. The soul that sins shall be cut off—the soul that sins purposefully, that doesn't use the opportunities given by manifestations in life. And what is the law of the Lord? "Thou shalt love the Lord thy God with all thy mind, thy body, thy soul, and thy neighbor—thy brother, thy friend, thy foe—as thyself." The whole law is in this. Ye can apply it to this or that extent, but do apply it in the whole law if ye would be at peace with self and know the peace which passeth understanding to a materially minded individual or world . . . The source of all life, and life in every form—whether it be in the vapor, the chemical motivative force as accredited to the vegetable, mineral or even the animal kingdom—is of one source, God. Make thyself, then, put thyself, be thyself, in companionship with Creative Forces. For the purpose is that each soul should be a co-creator with God. 4047-2

John 15:1

I am the real vine, and my Father is the gardener. (N.E.B.)

I am the true vine, and my Father is the husbandman. (A.V.)

I am the true vine, and my Father is the vinedresser. (C.B.)

For each experience in the earth is as a schooling, is as an experience for the soul. For how gave He? He is the vine and ye are the branches, or He *is* the source and ye are the trees. As the tree falls so does it lie. *There* it begins when it has assimilated, when it has applied in *spiritual* reaction that it has gained. 262-99

John 15:2

Every barren branch of mine he cuts away; and every fruiting branch he cleans, to make it more fruitful still. (N.E.B.)

Every branch in me that beareth not fruit he taketh away: and every branch that beareth fruit, he purgeth it, that it may bring forth more fruit. (A.V.)

Every branch of mine that bears no fruit, he takes away, and every branch that does bear fruit he prunes, that it may bear more fruit. (C.B.)

Remember, whom the Lord loveth He chasteneth, and purgeth every one; that they may bear fruit in the glorifying of His purpose with the children of men. 2934-1

Know that thy redeemer liveth, and as ye urge others remind them—as well as self—that what ye have and what ye are is by His grace and mercy and not by your own feeble efforts. For He withholdeth no good thing from those who love Him, and those He loveth He purgeth. Then, know that the material and mental sorrows are but the purging necessary that ye may indeed manifest the more His love in the earth. 3581-1

And he whom the Lord loveth He chasteneth, and purgeth every one; that they may bear fruit indeed in Him. Not such that the teeth of the children of men are set on edge by the sourness of their lives, but rather that there is the stimulation to activity.

Not neglectful of the little things, not unmindful of the humbleness necessary. Knowing He is not a respecter of persons. For he that is the greatest is indeed the servant of all. 1616-1

Fulfill that *thou knowest* to do in thine mind, in thine heart, in thine body; for the *Lord* loveth whom He testeth, and will purge every one—that you may be His companions with Him. What *is* a day of joy in the earth compared to an eternity of glory with thy Brother, the Christ? For by Him all things were made, and even as He has loved you, so may ye love Him—if ye will do His biddings. 262-69

John 15:3

You have already been cleansed by the word that I spoke to you. (N.E.B.)

Now ye are clean through the word which I have spoken unto you. (A.V.)

You are already made clean by the word which I have spoken to you. (C.B.)

For He *is* the way; He is the life; He is the vine and ye are the branches. Bear ye fruit, then, worthy of that thou hast chosen; and He will keep that thou hast committed unto Him against every experience that may be required, that may be needed, that may come in thine attempts to show forth the Lord's death till He come again; death meaning that transition, that decision, that change in every experience. For if ye die not daily to the things of the world ye are none of His.

Then, lift up thine hearts, thine minds, in praise to Him who has *given* thee the opportunity that ye may be as lights showing the way; reconsecrating thyself, thy service, thy joys, thy sorrows, to His service, that ye may have the greater joy, the greater blessings in Him. 262-73

John 15:4

Dwell in me, as I in you. No branch can bear fruit by itself, but only if it remains united with the vine; no more can you bear fruit, unless you remain united with me. (N.E.B.)

Abide in me, and I in you. As the branch cannot bear fruit of itself, except it abide in me. (A.V.)

Abide in me, and I in you. As the branch cannot bear fruit by itself, unless it abides in the vine, neither can you, unless you abide in me. (C.B.)

To Dwell in Him Is to Recognize Who We Are

To put these words into context with what I usually call "reality," I need to become aware that I—like the majority of the souls in the earth plane today—have been incarnated into the earth probably hundreds or thousands of times. Are we all slow learners, then, that we haven't yet become one with God? Haven't we gotten the idea yet? What does it mean to "dwell in Him"?

Sometimes one needs to follow the instructions that Cayce gave one individual. He told the man, first of all, to bring about the corrections of the physical body but, at the same time, to interpret in the temple of his own body the promises found in these chapters. For, Cayce not only saw the relationships between the illnesses of the body and the deviation from the very laws of life, but he also said that the analyzing of the truths that Jesus presented in the light of His ministry, "and the application of same in the lives of individuals is an individual experience. But the closer, the nearer one applies those tenets, those truths, those principles in one's daily experience, the greater is the ability of the mental and spiritual self, to revivify the physical activities of any given body." (2074-1) This means healing or regeneration of the body. This may be why Jesus could bring healing to any who asked, and even to those who were not asking—why He came to be called the Great Physician. For He was one with the Source of those tenets, those truths, and thus became the Source Himself.

The promise is seen in John 15:7: "If you dwell in me, and my words dwell in you, ask what you will, and you shall have it." There are no ifs, ands, or buts about it. This is a promise. You need to read this carefully, however, and not misinterpret it. And, as Cayce said several times, don't tell God when you want the promise fulfilled. The date lies within your own being.

Jesus said that He is the vine, we are the branches. We have no power to do as He did unless we stay one with the vine; unless we dwell with Him as the vine; unless we abide with Him. As branches, we do not gain energy or life from any other source. The pine tree does not give us life. The oak, mighty though it may be, does not. We can't be divided.

We cannot gain life from two sources at the same time. To manifest the abilities and oneness that Jesus had, we must choose Him and act in that way. Jesus said that He is the way, the truth, the life, and no one cometh to the Father but by Him. Cayce stated it a bit differently: "For He *is* the way, the truth. They that approach any other way become those that cheat themselves, robbing themselves of the truth that would bring the preventing of those things that separate man from the love of the Father." (2600-2)

The mind is always the builder, and it apparently has a relationship with the Christ in a special way. This is how Cayce once described it:

> *Live, be* in that awareness. Not that it is not ever to be made practical, daily. For, in a material world one's religion, one's spirituality must be *lived* rather than preached; yet in the mental awareness one may be *wholly* in that temple. For, thy body is indeed the temple of the living God. *There* He has promised to meet thee. Become aware of that indwelling in the holy of holies in thine own temple-self. For, the mind is the builder in the spiritual world. It is the way—even as He is the way. 2246-1

We need, then, to be aware of where our life originates, what part the Christ plays in it, and let go of our resistances, if we wish to dwell in Him and let His words dwell in us; a close communication that requires the use of our mind as the real builder. And we need to keep joyful, keep optimistic: "Pray, often; seeing, feeling, asking, desiring, expecting help—from Him; who is the way, the truth, the light. He faileth not those who keep His purposes." (2514-1)

> Keep then that thou hast purposed to do in relationships to thy desires in Christ, thy love in being a channel of blessings to others, thy activities in thy relationships with others.
>
> So may the spirit of truth, so may the Christ as He hath given abide in thee. For, "As ye abide in me, I in the Father, so may the world know the glory of the Father through *thy* activity among thy fellow man."
> 585-4

Then—in preparation of self—fear not. Let thy
mind, thy body, be consecrated, set aside, *determined* that "As the Lord wills, so may it be done,"
and that the Lord will have His way with thee; that
the words of thy mouth, the meditations of the
heart, may be acceptable in His sight; taking only
Him as thy guide who hath given, "If ye will abide in
me, I will abide in thee." 1089-2

John 15:5

**I am the vine, and you are the branches. He who
dwells in me, as I dwell in him, bears much fruit;
for apart from me you can do nothing. (N.E.B.)**

**I am the vine, ye are the branches: He that abideth
in me, and I in him, the same bringeth forth much
fruit: for without me ye can do nothing. (A.V.)**

**I am the vine, you are the branches. He who abides
in me, and I in him, he it is that bears much fruit,
for apart from me you can do nothing. (C.B.)**

There have been turmoils and strife from the anger of others, from the disappointments of self,
from conditions and experiences that have made
for fear at times to creep in—and the wonderments
as of how a loving Father allow one, that tries and
tries, to be in a position to suffer so in body, in mind,
as in the experience of the entity and those about it
at times. Yet, with the application of that which has
been held as the spiritual guidance in the sojourn
in the earth, there will come that saving grace, that
expression that is given by Him who is the author
and the finisher of faith, who *is* the life, who is the
way, who is the vine; "and ye as the branches" may

in Him find that He will abide with they that keep His commandments, and His grace is sufficient unto thee, and will keep and sustain thee even in those conditions that overwhelm thee at times, and bring thee to a greater knowledge and understanding in the light of that service He would have thee render in His vineyard. For the day dawns when the love of the Father is to be manifested more and more among men. Know that thou hast a part in same, and it will be given thee that thou shouldst do. In the selfsame *hour,* as ye have need of, will it be shown thee. 702-1

That as is held, *keep* that inviolate; knowing that there must be the ideal set before self that may only be accomplished in the *fulfillment* of the trusts as are given from time to time; for the Spirit suffers none to be tempted beyond that they are *able* to bear. Knowing, then, that such is, as to whether one is gratifying selfish interest, or is keeping spiritual faith, walk in that light as is set in Him who gave, "Follow in that way, for my yoke is easy and my burden is light, for in me is life, and the water of life, for I am the vine and ye are the branches. He that dwelleth in me dwelleth in the Father also." 853-1

John 15:6

He who does not dwell in me is thrown away like a withered branch. The withered branches are heaped together, thrown on the fire, and burnt. (N.E.B.)

If a man abide not in me, he is cast forth as a branch, and is withered; and men gather them, and cast them into the fire, and they are burned. (A.V.)

If a man does not abide in me, he is cast forth as a branch and withers; and the branches are gathered, thrown into the fire and burned. (C.B.)

Hence oft in the experience such opportunities come, such experiences—if there is kept the ideal in Him as the guide, the way, pointing out to self in the light of His understanding those experiences that become as stepping-stones to the way that leads to life in Him, the everlasting way; that manner, that understanding that makes for the arousing in the experiences of others the thinking more of the Divine within.

Thus, as the entity receives through those manners of expression in writings, in visions, in dreams—hold fast to that as He has set. *Weigh* them in the balance of that He has given as the balance for every soul. "Abide in me—and I in Him—and thus become one with the Lord of righteousness, of justice, of mercy, of love."

If those impulses become tinged with self-aggrandizement, or self-indulgences, they become as those things that are without the pall—and become stumbling-stones along the way of light. 540-3

John 15:7

If you dwell in me, and my words dwell in you, ask what you will, and you shall have it. (N.E.B.)

If ye abide in me, and my words abide in you, ye shall ask what ye will, and it shall be done unto you. (A.V.)

If you abide in me, and my words abide in you, ask whatever you will, and it shall be done for you. (C.B.)

But if there is set a definite period or manner of meditation, as may be given in a very close study of that which has been manifested or expressed through these sources and compiled in the paper on meditation, there may be had a balancing. And in the experiences of the entity there may come an activity that will enable the body-physical (as would be expressed from the material side alone) to "snap out" of these expressions, those depressions, those feelings of floating, those feelings of losing control, those feelings of the inability of concentration.

For, guided by those that are the Creative Forces in manifestation in a physical body, there may come not only for self but for humanity, for individuals, for groups, that which may be the *great* manifestation. And indeed may it be said that through the concentration, through the consecration of self, that as given of old may be fulfilled; "The glory of the Lord will be manifest among men, for I, thy God, hath spoken it."

Then—in preparation of self—fear not. Let thy mind, thy body, be consecrated, set aside, *determined* that "As the Lord wills, so may it be done," and that the Lord will have His way with thee; that the words of thy mouth, the meditations of the heart, may be acceptable in His sight; taking only Him as thy guide who hath given, "If ye will abide in me, I will abide in thee."

And He will give his angels charge concerning thee, and they will bear thee up—lest thou stumble and fall into materiality. 1089-2

John 15:8

This is my Father's glory, that you may bear fruit in plenty and so be my disciples. (N.E.B.)

Herein is my Father glorified, that ye bear much fruit; so shall ye be my disciples. (A.V.)

By this my Father is glorified, that you bear much fruit, and so prove to be my disciples. (C.B.)

For as ye do it unto the least, ye do unto thy Christ, thy God.

If thou art lax in thine undertakings, then thou art lax in thy duty, thy promises to thy Lord.

If thou art vexed with those that despitefully use thee, then thou hast met a shortcoming in those forces that would bring about fear in thine own experience.

But as ye follow along the way of showing forth those aptitudes and attitudes that are as a portion of the spirit of truth—patience, long-suffering, brotherly love—these will bring, these do bring, those things that make for harmony in thy experience with thy fellow man.

This is the way of the spirit. For the fruits of the spirit are that ye keep faith with thy Christ. 585-4

John 15:9-10

As the Father has loved me, so I have loved you. Dwell in my love. If you heed my commands, you will dwell in my love, as I have heeded my Father's commands and dwell in his love. (N.E.B.)

As the Father hath loved me, so have I loved you: continue ye in my love. If ye keep my commandments, ye shall abide in my love; even as I have kept my Father's commandments, and abide in his love. (A.V.)

As the Father has loved me, so have I loved you; abide in my love. If you keep my commandments, you will abide in my love, just as I have kept my Father's commandments and abide in his love. (C.B.)

What more wonderful can there be than to know that self's own ego, self's own I AM with the spirit of truth and life, has made aware within self that thou hast been called by name? Not another name, for there be no name under heaven whereby men may be saved than in His name! Then, as these awarenesses arise within thine inner self and thou seest thine own self, speak as with thy Lord and thy Master, and thou wilt come to hear more and more even as He has given, "If ye will but harken I will come and abide with thee." 707-2

John 15:11

I have spoken thus to you, so that my joy may be in you, and your joy complete. (N.E.B.)

These things have I spoken unto you, that my joy might remain in you, and that your joy might be full. (A.V.)

These things I have spoken to you, that my joy may be in you, and that your joy may be full. (C.B.)

So attune thyselves that ye may harken, not as to an experience only; but rather *live* and *be* the experience in the hearts of those that are seeking to find their way; whether in the troubles of the body, of the mind, or whether they are lost among those turmoils of the cry, "This way—That way"—Here and there. Be the experience to someone to light their lives, their bodies, their minds to thy *living* Lord, thy Brother, the Christ! For He has promised in His words in thine own heart, that keeps the hope, that keeps the fires of thine own heart aflame, "Ye finding me may know the *joy* of the Lord."

As many of you served there, as many experienced those purifications for an active service among their fellow man in an *individual* experience, so may ye purify thy minds and thy bodies, or purify thy *bodies* that thy *mind* may put *on* Christ, the garments of a living Lord, that ye may be not as ones stumbling, as ones fearful of this or that, but *sure* and *certain* in the joys of a risen Lord; that indeed thy body in its expressions may be the Temple *Beautiful* for thy *living* Lord.

He thy Brother, thy Christ, hath given that God is God of the *living* way! He *is* Life! He *is* Love. He *is* Beauty. He *is* Harmony. He *is* Music. He *is* the rhythm of the body in dance that is a service to thy God. Though others make slight of thy manner of speech, of thy body, of thy walks, of thy ways, hold fast to Him; grudging no one, loving all. For as given, in thy preparation, in the indication and the vindication in thine service there, *self* is lost in the love of thy fellow man through the joy of the Lord in thee. 281-25

John 15:12

This is my commandment: love one another, as I have loved you. (N.E.B.)

This is my commandment, That ye love one another, as I have loved you. (A.V.)

This is my commandment, that you love one another as I have loved you. (C.B.)

Let love be without dissimulation—that is, without *possession* but as in that manner as He gave, "Love one another, even as I have loved you"; willing to give the life, the self, for the purpose, for an ideal. Other than this, these become as that which will bring in the experience that in which each will hate self and blame the other. 413-11

In the love of the Father is all desire, all hope. And if ye will make His ways thy ways, then thy life, thy hopes, thy desires grow! For in giving happiness to others it grows in the giving. In finding peace within self ye are able to bring peace into the lives and the experiences of others. For God is not mocked, and as ye sow, so must ye reap. The Lord love thee, the Lord keep thee—in His ways! 262-116

As each gains, through their own meditation or prayer, that they may be known among men even as they are known with Him, this *takes* on an import. Would ye act before thy God in the manner ye act before thine brother? Love one another, "A new commandment I give, that ye *love* one another." In *this* manner may each see themselves as others see them. Let not thy words and thy actions be so different that they are not children of the same family. Let thy deeds, let thy words, be in keeping with that others see in thee. 262-9

Let thy purposes in thy dealings with others be kept in attune, in accord, with that new commandment He gave unto those about Him, "Love one another." And as thy activities bring those trials, those doubts, those fears, place them upon the altar of service; and the joy of the Lord will fill thee with peace, contentment, that comes to those who put their trust in Him. Be not afraid. God is not mocked; whatsoever one soweth, that—too—shall one reap. Condemn not, that ye be not condemned. Rather let thy life, in thy conversation—in thy invocation—keep thee close to Him. 281-50

John 15:13

There is no greater love than this, that a man should lay down his life for his friends. (N.E.B.)

Greater love hath no man than this, that a man lay down his life for his friends. (A.V.)

Greater love has no man than this, that a man lay down his life for his friends. (C.B.)

These do not become then theory—they do not become speculative; but as ye do them, so is it measured to thee again. For greater love hath no man than that he lay down his own self for those that he loves. And that alone that ye give, have given—of thy body, thy mind, thy strength—do ye possess. Just as He—as thy Guide, the Guard, thy *Hope*—has given Himself; so are ye His.

So as ye expend your body, your mind, your purposes, your desires, to bring to others the consciousness of His abiding presence, so may ye *know* His peace, so it may be thine as ye accept, as ye use, as ye apply same in thy relationships to thy fellow man day by day. 1662-1

For even as He taught, he that is willing to lay

down his life for a cause *gains* the cause!

Then as He gave Himself as a ransom for many, so may those who have embraced Him gain a concept of that for which He stands, and become active in that direction. Not for fame, not for fortune, not even for what may be termed a patriotic spirit—for or because of a wrong concept, but for those activities that are to bring the fruits of the Spirit; as hope, faith, love, long-suffering, brotherly kindness, gentleness, and most of all *patience.*

For in patience we become aware of that relationship with the Creative Forces, that may only be expressed in materiality in what we do to our fellow man. For, "As ye do it unto the least of thy brethren, ye do it unto me," saith He that *is* the way, the truth, the light! 1598-1

Let thy yeas be yea, thy nays be nay. "Let others do as they may, but for me I will serve a *living* God," who has shown in man—*all* men, everywhere—that image of the Creator, in that the soul may grow in grace, in knowledge, in peace, in harmony, in understanding.

Be ye doers of the word; not hearers only. Thus ye become the door that the *Way,* the Christ, the Savior, may enter in; for *He is* the way, the truth, and the light. 262-29

John 15:14-15

You are my friends, if you do what I command you. I call you servants no longer; a servant does not know what his master is about. I have called you friends, because I have disclosed to you everything that I heard from my Father. (N.E.B.)

Ye are my friends, if ye do whatsoever I command you. Henceforth I call you not servants; for the servant knoweth not what his lord doeth: but I have called you friends; for all things that I have heard of my Father I have made known unto you. (A.V.)

You are my friends if you do what I command you. No longer do I call you servants, for the servant does not know what his master is doing; but I have called you friends, for all that I have heard from my Father I have made known to you. (C.B.)

Jesus, the Christ, is the mediator. And in Him, and in the study of His examples in the earth, is *life*—and that ye may have it more abundantly. He came to demonstrate, to manifest, to give life and light to all.

Here, then, ye find a friend, a brother, a companion. As He gave, "I call ye not servants, but brethren." For, as many as believe, to them He gives power to become the children of God, the Father; joint heirs with this Jesus, the Christ, in the knowledge and in the awareness of this presence abiding ever with those who set this ideal before them. 357-13

John 15:16

You did not choose me: I chose you. I appointed you to go on and bear fruit, fruit that shall last; so that the Father may give you all that you ask in my name. (N.E.B.)

Ye have not chosen me, but I have chosen you, and ordained you, that ye should go and bring forth fruit, and that your fruit should remain: that whatsoever ye shall ask of the Father in my name, he may give it to you. (A.V.)

You did not choose me, but I chose you and appointed you that you should go and bear fruit and that your fruit should abide; so that whatever you ask the Father in my name, he may give it to you. (C.B.)

And when ye consider what disappointments ye have had in individual associations, think how thy God must have been disappointed in thee when thou hast spoken lightly of thy brother, when thou hast condemned him in thine own conscience, when thou has questioned as to the purpose of those hearts that sought in the light of the best that *they* understood—or that even used their abilities for the aggrandizing of their own selfish motives. Hast thou prayed with them? Hast thou spoken kindly with them? Might not their path have been shown in *thine* life that desire as He manifested when He thought it not robbery to be equal with God and to offer Himself, His life, His body, His desires, as a sacrifice for thee that thou in thine own self-glory, in thine own understanding, might come to a knowledge that the desires of the heart—if they are spiritualized in that thou livest the life He has shown thee—thou may have in thine experience that He has promised, "What ye ask in my name, believing, that may the Father give thee"? Why art thou impatient? For the carnal forces are soon given over to the lusts thereof, but the spirit is alive through eternity! Be not impatient, but love ye the Lord! 262-63

John 15:17

This is my commandment to you: love one another. (N.E.B.)

These things I command you, that ye love one another. (A.V.)

This I command you, to love one another. (C.B.)

Fear Blocks Our Inheritance

If you were to ask Jesus what you are to inherit, what do you think He would say? Eternal life, perhaps? He showed us how to obtain it, this that we call eternal life, by living a lifetime without error, without sin, manifesting the love that is the nature of the Creative Forces of the universe. All we need to do is follow in His footsteps, to be obedient, as we have already discussed. We need to be loving, don't we?

What if we have retained a certain amount of rebellion from the time when, by choice, we declared our independence and moved away from God. That is part of the Cayce story and seems to be inherently part of the biblical account of things. We *have* that power, and we can tell the Creator that we don't care what *He* wants, we want to do our own thing. This is the power of free will, and we were given that power when we were created as spiritual entities, *not* when we arrived on the earth.

In Jesus' parable of the prodigal son (Luke 15:11-32) that is what happened to this teenager. He wanted his inheritance, which in this case was money, and he said, in effect, "I'm going out to seek my fortune, my way of life, what I want to do—and it doesn't matter what you, my father, really want." With his power to make up his own mind, he did just that.

That wasn't the end of the story, of course. He found that, after all his money was gone, the only job he could get was feeding the swine in the farmer's field. He was near starvation, having only the husks that were to be fed to the hogs as his food. He was desperate.

Finally, he woke up. "Why did I leave my father's mansion? I have nothing. If I go home, will he accept me after all that I've done?" We know the story, of course. He was greeted while he was still a long way off and was given a feast and welcomed back home. He learned the hard way not to rebel but to accept love. He learned by observing his father, how important it is to forgive and understand. Perhaps we could say he grew up, he matured and became a worthy son to the father. Perhaps the older son who stayed home learned also the lesson of how to love and forgive through his father's actions.

Are you a son, a daughter of the Father, created in His image and finding yourself still in a foreign land, like the rest of us? Jesus was telling us a story that the deeper parts of ourselves understand better than the conscious mind, living in a world of matter, where we have lost contact with that mansion that the Father owns. And we are actually on the way back, following a path that was demonstrated by the Master, the Christ who became the Truth, the Life, the Light, the Way. Cayce said it like this: "For, as there is builded in the innate and manifested experience of each entity, these become at variance oft to that ordinarily comprehended. For, the awareness or consciousness in the material plane has been and is given an individual soul as an opportunity for growth; which has been indicated by Him who is the way, the truth, the light . . . " (2629-1)

We have been told that the other dimension is so much more beautiful, filled with Light beyond description—why, then, since we are still here, aren't we using every opportunity that we can to grow and to achieve that oneness with God?

One block, certainly, that we can recognize is fear, which keeps us from realizing what our inheritance is and from claiming it. Again, Edgar Cayce shared with us some of the wisdom from universal sources about fear and its nature: "Fear is as the fruit of indecisions respecting that which is lived and that which is held as the ideal. Doubt is as the father of fear. Remember, as He gave, 'He that asks in my name, doubting not, shall have; for I go to the Father.' If doubt has crept in, it becomes as the father of fear. Fear is as the beginning of faltering. Faltering is as that which makes for dis-ease throughout the soul and mental body." (538-33)

The fear may be imbedded in our unconscious minds because we feel that we can never make a perfect picture or live a perfect life in this dimension. But perhaps that is not what is intended nor stated. Jesus said simply that we are commanded to love one another, as He has loved us. He has loved us in daily activities, and we can do the same. In one reading, Cayce reminded us that "He thy Brother, thy Christ, hath given that God is God of the *living* way! He *is* Life! He *is* Love. He *is* Beauty. He *is* Harmony. He *is* Music. He *is* the rhythm of the body in dance that is a service to thy God." (281-25)

Let's find the fears disappearing as we dissipate the doubts and rest in the security that God will indeed care for us and answer us, no matter what the request may be. We need, however, to act as if we believe the promise will be fulfilled.

Help will come as we meditate regularly:

If the entity will enter into the silence with the divine influences thrown about self, that there may be no hindrances from outside influences that would possess or would direct, other than from that promise in Him, "As ye ask in my name, believing, so shall it be in thine experience," there may be the purification of self—as the entity surrounds self with that which is innately an expression of purification, of dedication, of making for an at-oneness with the purposes in Creative Forces and Energies—such that there may flow in and through and out to others that which has been the promise; that the laying on of hands, and the prayers of those that have found patience, may save many from the turmoils and strifes of a dis-ease in a material body. 823-1

As we move forward, moment by moment, in making reality out of these steps, we will gradually remove those blocks that keep us from claiming our inheritance.

So, in thine development, let those words be the echo of all that thou wouldst do, that in the name of the Father—through the love as shown in the Son— the life may be guided day by day in its walks before men; and thus may there come to this soul the harmonious influences that make for the life being more worthwhile in the expressions of same, as it goes about meeting the daily activities that come in the expressions of self, bringing glory, honor in thine self through the love the Father has shown in the sons of men.

For, as He has given, the new commandment comes unto every soul, "that ye love one another even as the Father hath loved you"; and love overcometh, love looketh not upon these things that are unlovely, it vaunteth not itself, it speaketh no evil, and begets love and friendship in *every* way and manner.

Thus in the expression of self in this experience to learn more of what love means in the manifestations of the acts of individuals *towards* its fellow man. 505-4

For, know—as ye do it unto the least of thy brethren, ye do it unto thy Maker. This is a law—a law of love, a law of justice, a law of mercy, a law of God. Embrace it. Make it thine, and thus fulfill thy place, thy ability to make known to others that love as was manifested in Him—who is the way, the truth, the light, the peace that may come to a troubled world about thee. Bring harmony to all, as thy presence does, as thy word does, to the consciousness of those about thee. But put the accent upon the peace *He* has promised, as His way, as His great commandment, "Love one another." 2400-1

. . . "A new commandment I give unto you, that ye love one another, that ye love thy neighbor as thyself, that *thou* would stand in thy neighbor's stead. Not to everyone that saith Lord, Lord, shall be called, but he that doeth the will of the Father." So in thine judgments, in the associations, he that doeth the will—or seeks to know the will, He may thy ways guide, He may thy acts manifested in His experience bring to the soul the knowledge of thy walks with thy God. Hence, as has been said, when thou prayest, let thy meditation be: "Use me, O God, as Thou seest I may better serve Thee; in my waking moments, in my walks and my dealings with my fellow man, be Thou the guide." 442-3

John 15:18

If the world hates you, it hated me first, as you know well. (N.E.B.)

If the world hate you, ye know that it hated me before it hated you. (A.V.)

If the world hates you, know that it has hated me before it hated you. (C.B.)

. . . and yet know, even as He gave, "Abiding in me—for if the world hated me, it will hate thee also for thy very goodness, for thy mercy, for thy grace," yet ye will have the abiding peace, if ye will abide in same, that will bring forth fruit *worthy* of acceptation by Him who is the Lord and the Judge of the earth. 1499-1

For as ye know, as ye interpret in thine own experience, as in the life of Him, who—though without fault—was hated of others. "If the world hate me, it does and it will hate thee." But if ye hate the world, if ye dislike those with whom ye are associated, then *His* death, His love, His promise becomes of none effect in thee!

For the *world* hath hated Him without a cause. Ye feel within thyself that ye are distrusted, that ye are hated without a cause. But if ye do the same in return, His promise becomes of none effect in thee— ye are of the world and not of Him. 3078-1

Let there be less and less resentment of any kind respecting others or in the apparent negligence on the part of others. Remember, as He has given, "If they have hated me they will hate you also—if they have misused me they will misuse you also." 3157-1

Begin with that in thine own life, as the pattern of thy life; not as something that is to be cloistered or that is to be lit and put under a bushel, but—as He gave—set it on the hill. Know you are right and don't fret because people say you are funny. They called Him funny, they called Him egotistical, they called Him blasphemous. If they loved Him not, they will not love thee. But in thyself, in thy body, thy mind, thy thoughts, thy activities, and—most of all—in

thy music, as ye practice even, see in each note a
voice, a song, a note of praise raised to Him, who is
the Giver of all good and perfect gifts, and who is
hurt when such gifts are used for indulgence, for
gratification, or in any respect not as glory to Him.
Not that this is selfish, for as it glorifies Him it is ever
as He gave, "And I, if I be lifted up, will draw all men
unto me." That means woman too, it means thee, in
that as ye glorify Him ye are fitted, ye are enabled to
raise others also. Thus ye contribute to that sphere
of activity about thee, to the glory of the Father in
the Christ. And He has promised to be with thee. He
keeps His promise. Then, it is necessary that you
keep yours—with yourself first, and those who love
you, who trust you, yea even with those who hate
you. Not because of them but because of Him, who
is the right. 3053-3

John 15:19

If you belonged to the world, the world would love
its own; but because you do not belong to the
world, because I have chosen you out of the world,
for that reason the world hates you. (N.E.B.)

If ye were of the world, the world would love his
own: but because ye are not of the world, but I have
chosen you out of the world, therefore the world
hateth you. (A.V.)

If you were of the world, the world would love its
own; but because you are not of the world, but I
chose you out of the world, therefore the world
hated you. (C.B.)

As ye have chosen me, so have I chosen you, that

ye may be a blessing to those who seek in *my* name to *know* the truth as may be magnified in *their* lives through *thine* aid in me. Grace, mercy and peace, is given to those thou asketh for in the proportion as thy trust, thy faith, is *in* me. As ye seek through raising in self that image of love in Him, so *may* thine self be lifted up, and the understanding comes *to* him who *seeks* for same . . .

Fear not that thine work will not find an outlet, once there is union of purpose. Has He not said, "Be joyous in that I have chosen *thee*, as *thou* hast chosen me and ye may be lights in *my* name"? 281-2

As the consciousness of the Christ presence comes nearer and nearer to thee, may ye be endowed with that of shedding *His* joy, *His* love into the life of others. The more knowledge, the more responsibility. The more love, the more ability. Keep thou the way open; for as He has chosen thee, so must ye choose His ways. For as He gave, "If ye love me, keep my commandments." 281-23

John 15:20

Remember what I said: "A servant is not greater than his master." As they persecuted me, they will persecute you; they will follow your teaching as little as they have followed mine. (N.E.B.)

Remember the word that I said unto you, The servant is not greater than his lord. If they have persecuted me, they will also persecute you; if they have kept my saying, they will keep yours also. (A.V.)

Remember the word that I said to you, A servant is not greater than his master. If they persecuted me,

they will persecute you; if they kept my word, they
will keep yours also. (C.B.)

How Do We Make Love a Living Thing?

We need to love! We need to love God, love our fellow
human beings, and love ourselves. This is the manner in
which we were created—the very image of God, but
somewhere along the way, we departed from the presence of that Source of all power, all life, all love. Never
mind how it happened—I think it was simple rebellion—
but it happened. We have the ability inside ourselves,
however, to choose and to awaken ourselves—and become aware of—that quality of love which still resides
within, the same power that was invested in us before
the worlds came into being.

As souls, we cannot, without loving, escape from the
hold the earth has on us and thus experience our oneness with God. Jesus recognized the Prince of this World,
the power of self, of sin, that typifies the earthly consciousness. And, as Cayce pointed out, "When the earth
came to be the dwelling place of sin, there came the
Son—that the earth and all therein might see, might
know, might experience, that the Son, the love of the Father, the glory of the Son might be manifested in flesh."
(262-82)

In living His life as the ultimate symbol of serving,
Jesus manifested love so we could know how it is to be
done. But we must realize that only we ourselves can
make love real in our lives. If Jesus had not spent several
incarnations in the earth meeting all the temptations
any of us might be faced with—so He could then come
as the manifestation of love and life, as the Christ—no
one could have known sin. Sin, as the separation from
God, is like darkness. Because the earth is to a great extent in darkness, light had to be manifested in the earth

as reality, as love, so that we could measure one against the other and choose.

That's why we need to love, having that knowledge that Jesus made it real through living the love He had to live.

If love is to become a necessary part of our lives, then we need to ask, "Well, exactly, what is love? How do I do it?" We say God is Love, but that begs the question for us. We don't truly comprehend the Universal Forces, the God Power, the Creative Forces. It is said that God is good, God is creative, but we know those same powers do exist within us if we choose to exercise them. But we are not God—and we are not love.

If we hate the world, we are not loving, and the promises we have been talking about are not for us. To love is to have less and less resentment toward others, no matter what they have done. Paul stated in the Bible that it is only in patience that we possess our souls—another difficult statement to understand fully.

After Paul had his experience on the road to Damascus, he did a turnaround in his life and became a force in the world in helping to create the Christian religion. He spoke about the fruits of the Spirit, indicating that these qualities of dealing with others were manifestations of the power of God, of the Christ, of Love, of the Spirit, moving through us and changing ourselves and others. Thus when we see ourselves (or others) being joyful, manifesting gentleness or patience in relationships with others, we know it is the Spirit of Life Itself, Love, that is moving through us and in us and affecting others beneficially in the process. Kindness, goodness, self-control, understanding, forgiveness—these and other qualities that produce inner peace and healing of the body are those that tell us we are in the light, not in darkness. That is, unless we slip. And we do that more often than we like. But we remember that God is a forgiving power.

The practice of loving comes about when we, in a sense, are not looking. A spouse, perhaps, sees us doing something around the house that reflects our desires. The response, when the action is discovered, is a caustic criticism. We would tend to start an argument, for there is that in all of us which wants to defend our way of doing things. But love shows up when we are able to be patient and understanding enough to say, "I didn't realize that you felt that way. Let's talk a little about it." The result of that kind of love is peace on earth, in a sense, instead of the war that might have come about.

Love is learned by stumbling, falling down, creating confusion in interpersonal relationships—until we learn that we can change those old habits of response and create the peace that passeth understanding. It is learned when we decide that we will really change our old habits and replace them with the love that is the nature of the Christ Consciousness. Being patient, over and over and over again, will make this happen. For we, looking deeply into our hearts, can gain what we desperately want, but the living of true love has to be done.

We all need this kind of metamorphosis, of course. But we must remember the purpose behind the change and what really happens during the process of manifesting love. Some people love so they may be loved in return. It's like giving a gift in order to receive something in recompense for the gift. If we are the ultimate object of the action, then it is self-service, not truly a loving or a forgiving gesture. If we, instead, see ourselves as channels or instruments of God's love in action, then we have indeed attuned our being to the God-Force, and the love is given in the same manner that Jesus mentioned: "Of myself I do nothing. It is the Father that worketh in me and through me that doeth the works." (John 8:28)

We might say, then, that all that is loving is simply being channeled through us, and we become loving ourselves in the process. That's how it happens.

Do not be misled in that that received is greater than the source from which the entity is acting as the medium for transmission of the truth or knowledge; for the servant is never greater than the master, though he may be equal with him. For, this is the birthright and the gift of the creative influence in this world! 355-1

Consider the Creative Forces, as to how they give life, light and immortality; and as to how He—who manifested same—fulfilled the law. Thinkest thou that thou are better than He? 1646-2

Remember this also, that though He were the Son, yet learned He obedience through the things which He suffered. Thou art not greater; thou art not better than He. Yet in Him ye may find relief, ye may find help. For hath He not given that where two or three persons in body, mind and soul agree toward anything, "Ask in my name of the Father, He will give it to thee"? These are sure promises. Not that this, a physical being, may be used to gratify only thine own heart or body but that the use of thy limbs may be to the glory of God. Hold thee this in mind, in meditation, in prayer, and how those ye love best in body, those who love thee best in body, are to pray, to meditate, to work with thee physically. 5348-1

John 15:21-22

It is on my account that they will treat you thus, because they do not know the One who sent me. If I had not spoken to them, they would not be guilty

of sin; but now they have no excuse for their sin. (N.E.B.)

But all these things will they do unto you for my name's sake, because they know not him that sent me. If I had not come and spoken unto them, they had not had sin: but now they have no cloak for their sin. (A.V.)

But all this they will do to you on my account, because they do not know him who sent me. If I had not come and spoken to them, they would not have sin; but now they have no excuse for their sin. (C.B.)

When the earth came to be the dwelling place of sin, there came the Son—that the earth and all therein might see, might know, might experience, that the Son, the love of the Father, the glory of the Son might be manifested in flesh. This is an illustration of how that ye are not tempted beyond that ye are able to bear. It hath been said again, "*God* hath at no time tempted man." But again as the Master hath said, "Had I not come ye would not have *known* sin." Hence man in his awareness of sin, of the Christ Spirit, of that which makes him in all the phases of his experience awakened to that, may become aware of God's destiny for the soul. Shall it return empty-handed or bearing *thy* name? 262-82

John 15:23

He who hates me, hates my Father. (N.E.B.)

He that hateth me hateth my Father also. (A.V.)

He who hates me hates my Father, also. (C.B.)

Analyze self as to purposes, as to intents—as in comparison with that for which He came into the earth. For, each entity—and this in particular—must find, even as He, that in the doing for others there comes the answer to the problems for self; in every direction.

For, as has been given, though He were the Son—even He learned obedience.

So may we, each, as individuals, gain the better understanding, the better way of material and mental application, by that study of self in relationships to our purposes, our intents being in keeping with that manifested by Him.

As was given of old, if He had not come, many would not have known sin; yea, none would have known sin. If He had not come, many would not have known—yea, none—complete righteousness.

So we each in our lives bring those problems in the experiences of those we meet day by day; thus forming that pattern, that activity in the lives of others, that brings the complete awareness of each soul's ability to be in at-onement with Him.

Thus atonement, at-onement, attunement becomes as one in intent, in purpose, in desire, in activity. 2174-3

John 15:24

If I had not worked among them and accomplished what no other man has done, they would not be guilty of sin; but now they have both seen and hated both me and my Father. (N.E.B.)

If I had not done among them the works which

none other man did, they had not had sin; but now
have they both seen and hated both me and my
Father. (A.V.)

If I had not done among them the works which no
one else did, they would not have sin; but now
they have seen and hated both me and my Father.
(C.B.)

How again hath He given? Ye had not known sin
unless the Son had come and shown thee the Way.
This is then the Wisdom that is shown in the life, in
the experience of each soul. It is through the varia-
tions, through those activities that make for the
thinking, the analyzing, the seeking for God and
God's wisdom, that man is brought to the closer
understanding; making for that consciousness
within the experience of each soul that in patience,
in long-suffering, in brotherly love, is wisdom. Yet
as judged by man in the earth, and of the earth, becomes as that which is weakness. But the weakness
of man is the wisdom of God. Just as the knowledge
of God, the wisdom of God applied in the daily experience of individuals, becomes strength, power,
beauty, love, harmony, grace, patience, and those
things that—in the lives of those who are applying
same—make for a life experience that is worthwhile, even in the turmoils of the earth and those
activities of sin and sorrow and shame and want
and degradation; as worthwhile experiences, that
the glory of the Father in the Son may become
known and read and seen and understood by others—that would take counsel of that ye *are* in thy
daily activity in the earth. 262-104

John 15:25

However, this text in their Law had to come true: "They hated me without reason." (N.E.B.)

But this cometh to pass, that the word might be fulfilled that is written in their law, They hated me without a cause. (A.V.)

It is to fulfill the word that is written in their law, They hated me without a cause. (C.B.)

As was said of old, a people hated without a cause; yet when that cause presented *prejudice*, then only enlarged upon those shortcomings, bringing to the forefront of the forces as were set in motion by same those same misinterpretations and misapplications of the power as is endowed the peoples as a peoples. Let then that which has been presented remain in the inner self as that which is true in its first sense, and build upon that which will be presented to self from time to time. 900-399

Then there is little need for attempting to heal an ill body unless the mind, the purpose, the ideal of the entity is set in Him who is peace, life, hope and understanding. For He is indeed the way and the truth and the light.

If the entity will apply in self that it *knows* to do— not as something that applies to self alone, but that applies to self in its relationships to others—the results will be apparent. Ye *apply* thy love, if ye would have others love thee! Ye do trust others and ye *are* the trust and the hope, if ye would have hope or expect others to have hope and trust in thee!

For as ye know, as ye interpret in thine own expe-

rience, as in the life of Him who—though without
fault—was hated of others. "If the world hate me, it
does and it will hate thee." But if ye hate the world,
if ye dislike those with whom ye are associated, then
His death, His love, His promise becomes of none
effect in thee!

For the *world* hath hated Him without a cause. Ye
feel within thyself that ye are distrusted, that ye are
hated without a cause. But if ye do the same in return, His promise becomes of none effect in thee—
ye are of the world and not of Him. 3078-1

John 15: 26-27

**But when your advocate has come, whom I will
send you from the Father—the Spirit of truth that
issues from the Father—he will bear witness to me.
And you also are my witnesses, because you have
been with me from the first. (N.E.B.)**

**But when the Comforter is come, whom I will send
unto you from the Father, even the Spirit of truth,
which proceedeth from the Father, he shall testify
of me: and ye also shall bear witness, because ye
have been with me from the beginning. (A.V.)**

**But when the Counselor comes, whom I shall send
to you from the Father, even the Spirit of truth, who
proceeds from the Father, he will bear witness to
me; and you also are witnesses, because you have
been with me from the beginning. (C.B.)**

The I Am Presence, that is all-knowing within
self, as has just been pointed out in the experiences
of the entity, is as set forth by Him—in the 14th,
15th, 16th and 17th of John; that it, the I Am, must

be motivated *by* the Father, God. Even as He gave, "I in thee, I in the *Father,* that ye may be glorified, that ye may *know all* that has been—for ye were with me—*from the beginning.*"
There is a slight variation.

Hold to that which the God-within directs, that is a manifestation even as the water activity—it answers to that within that keeps, creates that balance; that answers to the manifestations of that *His* experience in the earth means to the whole of they that take hold upon God to *do* His will in the earth!

Q. If God is impersonal force or energy—

A. [Interrupting] He *is* impersonal; but as just been given, so *very* personal! It is not that ye deal only with *impersonal*—it is *within and without!* It is *in* and *without,* and only as God *quickeneth* the spirit within, by the use, by the application of the God-force within to mete it out to others. Else *how, why,* did that material experience of a man hanging on a cross bring—*bring*—redemption to a world? In this:

Though ye know He had the power . . . to heal, though He had power to rid the very taking *hold* upon death, it had no claims upon Him. Why? *Quickened* by the Father because the life *lived* among men, the dealings among *men,* brought *only* hope, *only* patience, *only* love, *only* long-suffering!

This then being the law of God made manifest, He *becomes* the law by manifesting same before man; and thus—as man, even as ye—becomes as one with the Father.

For until ye become in purpose, in activity, a savior—yea, a god—unto thy fellow man, ye do not take hold upon that *personality,* the *individuality* of *God*—that is the life, that is the being of life, eternity, hope and love!

These then become not only as impersonal but personal, in that ye know thyself, even as He—thy brother in the flesh—made manifest that ye are aware of thyself *being* thyself, yet one with Him; and thus able to enter into the joys, *wholly,* that are prepared since—yea, before—the very foundations of materiality, for those that keep His ways. 1158-12

Take that thou hast in hand, that thou hast builded day by day, and without fear *open* the door that He may come in and abide with thee; for "He that takes my yoke upon him and learns of me, with *him* will I abide day by day, and all things will be brought to remembrance that I have given thee since the foundations of the world, for thou were with me in the beginning and thou may abide with me in that day when the earth will be rolled as the scroll; for the heavens and the earth will pass away, but my word shall *not* pass away." The promises in Him are sure—the way ye know! 262-28

4

The Gospel of John, Chapter 16

"I have told you all this to guard you against the breakdown of your faith." (John 16:1)

If Jesus is talking to you (or me), as Cayce seemed to be saying so many times, several questions immediately come to mind when we read His statement in the first verse of this chapter. First, what causes a breakdown in our faith? Then, do words guard us against destruction or breakdown or a disruption of that quality which we know is so very important in our relationship with the Divine? Is it the words or the application of some of these instructions which we've been given?

After all, it is our choice what we do in this earth. If we act, believing—even though our belief factor is slim and weak—the faith will grow strong with every step, every act. Or do we say we believe these promises, but act like we don't, allow ourselves to be always questioning, wondering if, in reality, this protection, this power is ours to use in designing our life?

It is our choice, in difficult situations, to act completely enough that we can say, with unquestioning sincerity, "I truly believe, I truly have faith in God and His goodness and in the Christ, who gave me all these promises, and I have acted in that manner, so that I know I have the power of the Christ Consciousness guarding my way through life."

With the belief, however—no matter how well it is safe-guarded—there come difficulties, tribulations, trials, and hostility. If Cayce is right in telling us that Jesus is talking to us, in these chapters, then there are to be those troubles for us just as there were for His disciples some two thousand years ago.

There has always been that battle between the dark forces and those powers that bespeak of the Light and Life. Even today, we are often wounded—not killed for our beliefs as the disciples were for theirs—but hurt here and there, distracted from the path on which our beliefs would lead us. In this way, what we have learned and practiced is guarding us so that our faith may not be shaken. Sometimes, it is very difficult. History is replete with instances where those who held to their deepest beliefs were jailed, dishonored, and sometimes killed.

It is hard to believe in a God of love and in His Son, when so much that is "evil" abounds in the earth. But the need is still there to believe in that which we cannot see with our three-dimensional senses.

There were fewer Cayce readings given that relate to John 16 and 17 than for the preceding two chapters. Frequently Cayce mentioned, however, the need to live these concepts day by day. When we recall that we can act only in this very moment—not a minute ago nor two minutes after this—we then need to use that perspective when we have an opportunity to act in a situation in our daily life—or think—in a way that is loving. The alternative is to act in an unloving manner. There is no real neutral ground, and there is no avoiding the action.

When we simply put our whole being in neutral, so to speak, not choosing one way or the other, we have probably arrived at the point in time that is described in the Revelation of John: "To the angel of the church at Laodicea write: 'These are the words of the Amen, the faithful and true witness, the prime source of all God's creation: I know all your ways; you are neither hot nor cold. How I wish you were either hot or cold! But because you are lukewarm, neither hot nor cold, I will spit you out of my mouth." (Revelation 3:14-16)

Cayce's readings understandably remind one of the Bible—since he was such an avid reader of the whole text. So he urged many to "Do something, even if it is wrong." It seems that action is what this earth was created for. We need to be in action, doing things.

However, it is not *what* we do that is so important, but rather *how* we do it. If we are moving, if we are acting, we must answer the question of *how* we are doing/acting/ thinking in our lives that moment. Are we loving to others and to ourselves as we move in consciousness? If not, then we are missing the opportunity of the moment. For it is when we love the other person, when we are gentle, forgiving, understanding that we move forward on the path of spiritual growth toward oneness with God, oneness with the Christ.

When Jesus was with His disciples, it was undoubtedly difficult for them to think of His dying. They could hardly conceive of His not being greater than any other human being, and for Him to be leaving was unthinkable. Then, for them to keep on when He was gone—what could they do without their Master, their Christ?

Today, we have not had contact with the physical entity called Jesus. Many have seen Him at a psychic level, in dreams or visions, or in meditation, or even in a desperate life-threatening situation. But not as the disciples saw Him, touched Him, and ate their meals with Him. Our faith may be more difficult to grasp, but the tribulations we face may not be as drastic either.

This chapter is dealing with this dilemma in the lives of those people of the New Testament—and with those of us who do believe, but who can only grasp the concept of Jesus existing today in another dimension, not walking the streets and sidewalks of our hometowns.

His prediction about leaving this world, however, led Him into talking about fulfilling His purpose as He goes to the Father, which His friends did not understand at the time either. But that's our challenge today, trying to understand this very difficult concept—that His purpose was to overcome the earth and thus become the Savior of all those who are involved in repeated incarnations on the earth.

How many of us understand what that really means for more than five billion individuals? It's understandable if we don't, when even His own disciples couldn't totally comprehend the enormity of the task. But there it is, and we are told in the Bible and in these readings that this is the fact. Do we believe? Perhaps that safeguarding of our faith in the Christ and His promises needs desperately to be there.

The presence of the Holy Spirit, the Comforter, as a result of Jesus' departing from His disciples and the earth plane, is explained by His simply saying that the Counselor would not come unless He left. Cayce pointed out it was not just the passing of the individual as in death, but rather it was the moving of the very spirit that actually brought the earth and all of materiality into existence as a *thing,* as a condition, for the souls and spirits and minds of humanity! "And thus *He is* the way, as He is the mind, and without Him there is no other way." (1947-1)

John 16:1-3

I have told you all this to guard you against the breakdown of your faith. They will ban you from the synagogue; indeed, the time is coming when anyone who kills you will suppose that he is performing a religious duty. They will do these things because they do not know either the Father or me. (N.E.B.)

These things have I spoken unto you, that ye should not be offended. They shall put you out of the synagogues: yea, the time cometh, that whosoever killeth you will think that he doeth God service. And these things will they do unto you, because they have not known the Father, nor me. (A.V.)

I have said all this to you to keep you from falling away. They will put you out of the synagogues; indeed, the hour is coming when whoever kills you will think he is offering service to God. And they will do this because they have not known the Father, nor me. (C.B.)

John 16:4

I have told you all this so that when the time comes for it to happen you may remember my warning. I did not tell you this at first, because then I was with you. (N.E.B.)

But these things have I told you, that when the
time shall come, ye may remember that I told you
of them. And these things I said not unto you at the
beginning, because I was with you. (A.V.)

But I have said these things to you, that when their
hour comes you may remember that I told you of
them. I did not say these things to you from the
beginning, because I was with you. (C.B.)

John 16:5-7

But now I am going away to him who sent me.
None of you asks me "where are you going?" Yet
you are plunged into grief because of what I have
told you. Nevertheless, I tell you the truth: it is for
your good that I am leaving you. If I do not go, your
Advocate will not come, whereas if I go, I will send
him to you. (N.E.B.)

But now I go my way to him that sent me; and none
of you asketh me, Whither goest thou? But because
I have said these things unto you, sorrow hath
filled your heart. Nevertheless I tell you the truth;
It is expedient for you that I go away: for if I go not
away, the Comforter will not come unto you; but if
I depart, I will send him unto you. (A.V.)

But now I am going to him who sent me; yet none
of you asks me, Where are you going? But because
I have said these things to you, sorrow has filled
your hearts. Nevertheless I tell you the truth; it is
to your advantage that I go away, for if I do not go
away, the Counselor will not come to you; but if I
go, I will send him to you. (C.B.)

Love Made Him the Savior of the World

If you will read again the reading selections (413-3 and 2970-1) found immediately following John 14:18, the statement made above becomes a bit more clear, more understandable. How could a man experiencing death by crucifixion become savior of not only a small group of people but of the whole of humankind? It's a mystery, certainly, but all mysteries exist as such until time, events, and knowledge—even of the spiritual realm—offer an explanation.

Part of the answer, perhaps, can be gained if one accepts the statement that God is Love, yet He is also the power of creativity, the source of life, the meaning of all creation and, in a real sense, of all that exists.

The oneness of the Father with Jesus and with you or me is demonstrated as often as each of us "will *let,* will desire, will make self a channel for the expressions of that love which *made* Him the Savior of men." Jesus showed us the way, became the way, and became the perfect expression of the love of the Father—all that exists.

The way to oneness with God could not be discerned prior to Jesus' birth. It could not be understood in the physical world without it being demonstrated in life itself by someone, some soul. It was finally accomplished by Him who became the Anointed One—the Christ— Jesus. So, in living that Divine Love throughout His life and His death—in overcoming the earth—Jesus became the Savior of the whole world.

He showed us the way to regain that oneness with God that we had when we were brought into being. After coming into being, we rebelled in wanting our own way. Since we chose, we certainly had the power to gain our own way. In that act, we removed ourselves from the presence of the Creator. The earth was formed for us, so we could go on a journey and prove that we were willing to learn how to love as God loves. We, in a sense, then, must be saved from the earth consciousness, which is evidenced by the statement that "I want my way—I want those things that are *mine.*"

All of us are in the flesh as He was, made so that we also could become one with the Divine, able to do all that He did. Thus He was the Way (to live our lives), the Truth (to guide us in our lives), the Light or the Life itself (for us to choose as our Ideal). For we were given the power of choice when God created us as souls. Over the centuries we have chosen this or that, and at a deep level we have chosen to love or not to love. We have chosen life or death, good or evil. Moses taught us: "Today I offer you the choice of life and good, or death and evil." (Deut. 30:15) Read the thirtieth chapter of Deuteronomy to gain the full sense of how love was taught as far back as the Bible records things.

How, then, might we do this that will bring us the assurance that He will indeed not leave us comfortless, will be with us to the end? The way is not difficult to find: first, we have to learn how to believe in the goodness of God and in the love which He truly is—and then, simply to make ourselves channels for that love that Jesus manifested, moment by moment.

> . . . as ye sow, so shall ye reap . . . sow the seeds of friendships, of love, of patience, of long-suffering, of kindness, of grace; and ye will find more and more that life and its dealings with others become worthwhile—beauty and the joy of living becomes part of the experience. And more and more will the love be poured out to thee, for His promises are sure—that as ye sow the seeds of righteousness, the seeds of the spirit of truth, "I and the Father will come and make our abode with thee—to do thee good." 1765-2

How do we understand better how the Father and the Christ might dwell with us—make their abode with us? Perhaps the Spirit of God (which brought us into being and is already in us) and the Spirit of the Christ (who came to show us the way and is the way) become one with our spirit (which is our soul or part of our soul) when we simply love one another.

Even though we have had the way shown to us, it is still difficult to follow, for we are reminded that what we find—what we see—in our fellow human beings is a reflection of what we understand the Creative Forces of the universe to actually be. So we must look with discernment for the truth, and we must act in a loving, gentle way in order for that abode to be a continuing reality.

For as He gave, "If I go not away the spirit of truth cometh not." What meaneth this? Not merely the passing. For it was the moving of the spirit that brought materiality into existence as a *thing*, as a condition, for the souls and spirits and minds of men! And thus *He is* the way, as He is the mind, and without Him there is no other way. 1947-1

Not that self, thine own ego may be satisfied, but rather that the spirit of truth—as exemplified in the manner, the way the Master, thy Savior did manifest—may be *through thee* manifested before and toward thy fellow man. For it was spoken of Him that He went about doing good. *No* one could speak evil of Him, yet *we* say, *ye* say, evil was done Him. Yet He said, "for that purpose came I into the world, that I might overcome the world," and thus that the glory of the Father, of the Creator—yea, of thy Elder Brother—might be manifest.

As has been declaimed by a teacher, there is one glory of the sun, another of the moon, another of

the stars; each differing in their glory according to
the purpose for which they each have been established. For what? That man might in himself see the
glory of the Father being made manifest by they
each performing their purpose in *their* coopera-
tion, in *their* activity, before Him.

So, in thine own life, in thine own relation, in
thine own associations one with another, how
speakest *thou*—how readest thou? that ye do this or
that in order that ye may be well thought of? or are
ye fearful of what another will say because thou art
called to do this or that? 262-94

So in choosing thine self in the ways to go, these
that are as influences are but as signposts, knowing
that thou hast passed this or that test, even as He
passed through the garden, the cross, the grave,
hell, and rose in the *newness* of all being put *under*
submission; for having overcome He *became* the
way, the light, the *Savior.* So, in those experiences
that would overcome, as He has given, when ye are
beset by those forces that would unbalance, unroot
thee from that thou hast believed, even as He, "Get
thee behind me, Satan, for thou savorest of the
things that are of the earth." 288-30

In the overcoming, then, He *is* the way, the manner in which individuals may become aware of their
souls that are in accord with that as may be one with
the spirit of truth; for corruption inherits not eternal life. The Spirit is the true life. Then, as individuals become aware of that ability *in Him* to be the
way, so they become the door, as representatives,
as agents, as those that present the way; and the
door is thus opened; and not to the man but the
spirit of self that bears witness with the spirit of

truth through Him that overcame the world, thus putting the world under His feet.

So we as heirs of the kingdom, as brothers one with Him, may enjoy that privilege as He has given to those that hear His voice and put on the whole armor; that we may run the race that is set before us, looking to Him, the author, the giver of light; for in Him ye live and move and *have* [your] being. Do ye become rebels? Do ye find fault one with another, that are as self heirs to that kingdom? Rather be in that humbleness of spirit, that His will "be done in earth as it is in heaven." Thus do we become the children of the Father, the door to the way, and joint heirs with Him in glory. 262-29

As is understood then—Father-God is as the body, or the whole. Mind is as the Christ, which is the way. The Holy Spirit is as the soul, or—in material interpretation—purposes, hopes, desires. 1747-5

John 16:8-11

When he comes, he will confute the world, and show where wrong and right and judgement lie. He will convict them of wrong, but their refusal to believe in me; he will convince them that right is on my side, by showing that I go to the Father when I pass from your sight; and he will convince them of divine judgement, by showing that the Prince of this world stands condemned. (N.E.B.)

And when he is come, he will reprove the world of sin, and of righteousness, and of judgment: of sin, because they believe not on me; of righteousness, because I go to my Father, and ye see me no more;

of judgment, because the prince of this world is judged. (A.V.)

And when he comes, he will convince the world concerning sin and righteousness and judgment; concerning sin, because they do not believe in me; concerning righteousness, because I go to the Father, and you will see me no more; concerning judgment, because the ruler of this world is judged. (C.B.)

For know, there is only *one Spirit*—that is the Spirit of Truth that has growth within same! For if there is the spirit of strife, or the spirit of any activities that bring about contention or turmoils, it takes hold upon those very fires that ye have so *well* put away; yet that keep giving, giving—urges that are spoken of, even as He that ye *know,* that the prince of this world is as a raging lion, going about seeking whom he may destroy! 1472-3

John 16:12

There is still much that I could say to you, but the burden would be too great for you now. (N.E.B.)

I have yet many things to say unto you, but ye cannot bear them now. (A.V.)

I have yet many things to say to you, but you cannot bear them now. (C.B.)

John 16:13-15

However, when he comes who is the Spirit of truth, he will guide you into all the truth; for he will not

speak on his own authority, but will tell only what
he hears; and he will make known to you the things
that are coming. He will glorify me, for everything
that he makes known to you he will draw from
what is mine. All that the Father has is mine, and
that is why I said, "Everything that he makes
known to you he will draw from what is mine."
(N.E.B.)

Howbeit when he, the Spirit of truth, is come, he
will guide you into all truth: for he shall not speak
of himself; but whatsoever he shall hear, that shall
he speak: and he will show you things to come. He
shall glorify me: for he shall receive of mine, and
shall show it unto you. All things that the Father
hath are mine: therefore said I, that he shall take of
mine, and shall show it unto you. (A.V.)

When the Spirit of truth comes, he will guide you
into all the truth; for he will not speak on his own
authority, but whatever he hears he will speak, and
he will declare to you the things that are to come.
He will glorify me, for he will take what is mine and
declare it to you. (C.B.)

For as He hath given, "As ye do it unto others, ye
do it unto me" . . . He *is* the Giver of all good and perfect gifts. Man may sow, man may act in the material manifestations of the spiritual forces that move
in matter; yet the returns, the increase, must come
from and through Him that *is* the gift of life. It is not
a consideration as to where or even how the seed of
truth in Him is sown; for *He* gives the increase if it is
sown in humbleness of spirit, in sincerity of purpose, with an eye-single that He may be glorified in

and among thy fellow man. *This* is the way; this is the manner that *He* would have thee go. 849-11

John 16:16

"A little while, and you see me no more; again a little while, and you will see me." (N.E.B.)

A little while, and ye shall not see me; and again, a little while, and ye shall see me, because I go to the Father. (A.V.)

A little while, and you will see me no more; again a little while, you will see me. (C.B.)

John 16:17-19

Some of his disciples said to one another, "What does he mean by this: 'a little while, and you will not see me, and again a little while, and you will see me,' and by this: 'Because I am going to my Father' "? So they asked, "What is this 'little while' that he speaks of? We do not know what he means." Jesus knew that they were wanting to question him, and said, "Are you discussing what I said: 'A little while, and you will not see me, and again a little while, and you will see me' "? (N.E.B.)

Then said some of his disciples among themselves, What is this that he saith unto us, A little while, and ye shall not see me: and again, a little while, and ye shall see me: and, Because I go to the Father? They said therefore, What is this that he saith, A little while? we cannot tell what he saith. Now Jesus knew that they were desirous to ask him, and said unto them, Do ye enquire among yourselves of that I said, A little while, and ye shall not see me: and again, a little while, and ye shall see me? (A.V.)

Some of his disciples said to one another, What is this that he says to us, A little while, and you will not see me, and again a little while, and you will see me; and, because I go to the Father? They said, What does he mean by a little while? We do not know what he means. Jesus knew that they wanted to ask him; so he said to them, Is this what you are asking yourselves, what I meant by saying, A little while, and you will not see me, and again a little while, and you will see me? (C.B.)

John 16:20

In very truth I tell you, you will weep and mourn, but the world will be glad. But though you will be plunged in grief, your grief will be turned to joy. (N.E.B.)

Verily, verily, I say unto you, That ye shall weep and lament, but the world shall rejoice; and ye shall be sorrowful, but your sorrow shall be turned into joy. (A.V.)

Truly, truly I say to you, you will weep and lament, but the world will rejoice; you will be sorrowful, but your sorrow will turn into joy. (C.B.)

John 16:21

A woman in labour is in pain because her time has come; but when the child is born she forgets the anguish in her joy that a man has been born into the world. (N.E.B.)

A woman when she is in travail hath sorrow, because her hour is come: but as soon as she is delivered of the child, she remembereth no more the anguish, for joy that a man is born into the world. (A.V.)

When a woman is in travail she has sorrow, because her hour has come; but when she is delivered of the child, she no longer remembers the anguish, for joy that a child is born into the world. (C.B.)

John 16:22

So it is with you: for the moment you are sad at heart; but I shall see you again, and then you will be joyful, and no one shall rob you of your joy. (N.E.B.)

And ye now therefore have sorrow: but I will see you again, and your heart shall rejoice, and your joy no man taketh from you. (A.V.)

So you have sorrow now, but I will see you again and your hearts will rejoice, and no one will take your joy from you. (C.B.)

John 16:23

When that day comes you will ask nothing of me. In very truth I tell you, if you ask the Father for anything in my name, he will give it you. (N.E.B.)

And in that day ye shall ask me nothing. Verily, verily, I say unto you, Whatsoever ye shall ask the Father in my name, he will give it you. (A.V.)

In that day you will ask nothing of me. Truly, truly, I say to you, if you ask anything of the Father, he will give it to you in my name. (C.B.)

John 16:24

So far you have asked nothing in my name. Ask and you will receive, that your joy may be complete. (N.E.B.)

Hitherto have ye asked nothing in my name: ask, and ye shall receive, that your joy may be full. (A.V.)

Hitherto you have asked nothing in my name; ask, and you will receive, that your joy may be full. (C.B.)

Ask, That Your Joy May Be Full

There are so many times when life in its apparent fullness fails to excite us, fails to bring us happiness, and we easily become despondent, depressed. It is then that we wonder—since we have already prayed and discussed with God how good we have been and how much we have helped our fellow humans—"Why has this happened to me? What have I done? Where have I missed the boat?" It seems as if God has departed from our presence. He has left us.

But then we remember what we have been told so many times. "God has never left you. If He is not there, guess who moved?" We really are never alone, even though it sometimes feels like it. There is always hope, wherever there is life. People who are ill need that assurance. People who are "well" sometimes need to be reminded that we are all ill in some of our ways and in parts of our being. We all need that assurance.

The disciples were fishermen, tax collectors, etc. They had been with Jesus these three years and had seen and experienced His remarkable ability to be one with God; to heal the sick, to bring life back to Lazarus. They had heard all His discourses, seen Him walk on water, do things no other human had done. Now, at this point in time, He tells them something they simply cannot understand. What does He mean, a little while and we won't see Him, and then a little while and we will see Him? What is this?

Jesus was able to read their minds, of course, as He still does—being part of each of us in ways that foil our visual senses. But His answer was not direct. Rather, He told them that they would be weeping, sorrowful, and hopeless at first, after He was crucified, but the sorrow would be turned to joy. In the twentieth through the twenty-fourth verses, He reminded them that it is like when a child is born. The mother is in labor—it hurts, and women understandably often cry or scream. But when the child is born, the parents are joyful, exuberant, celebrating, and see the world in a new light. So it would be with the disciples. And so it is with us, if Jesus is really talking to us. The crucifixion was a terrible thing and is still that to us today. But the change in the world because Jesus—in a mysterious way—took the sins of the world upon Him to the cross has brought joy to all of those who feel these realities within their beings and believe that it happened that way.

Then Jesus told them that a new relationship had come about, in that they no longer needed an intermediary in order to talk with God or ask whatever they might from the Creator. They needed only to ask in Jesus' name, and it would become so, and the joy would be a constant part of their lives.

Read those verses again and then the readings that follow. It becomes clearer that it may be simply the belief that one holds in the promises, as well as living a life that conforms to those beliefs (that we are certainly able to live)—just to be kind, to be gentle, to be patient with others day by day. This in itself is the fulfillment of a promise that fits us to approach the throne of grace and mercy and ask what we will of God, and it will be answered—if we follow the rules, and we have been exploring those during these pages—then our joy may indeed be full.

. . . for He hath knowledge of that we have need of before we ask, but "Ask and ye shall receive." As ye know to give gifts of love, mercy, patience, with thine fellow man, even though they wrong thee in act or word, how much *more* doth thy heavenly Father give to them that ask Him. Let thine purpose be in expressing, in manifesting, His power. All praises give unto Him! Not in what I did, we did, or the other! The praise, the power, is in Him. 281-9

Ask and ye shall receive, saith the Lord who is thy keeper. Then in thy prayer, thy meditation, call ye on Him. For He is not afar off. And with the spirit of love that is His commandment to thee, "that ye love one another" ask in His name.

Sow the seeds of truth, but *do not* continue to scratch them up—but leave the results, the increase to Him.

Sow that as ye would have thy Father do, and say, to thee. 262-118

Live closer to Him, who giveth all good and perfect gifts, and ask and ye shall receive; knock and it shall be opened unto you. Give and it shall be returned fourfold. Give, give, give, if you would receive. There has never been the lack of necessities,

neither will there be, so long as adhering to the
Lord's way is kept first and foremost. 254-11

Q. How may I come to a fuller realization of my
oneness with God?
A. The more ye walk, the closer ye walk with that
promise "I come—as ye ask ye will receive; if ye knock
it will be opened," but it must be for the manifestation of His divine love in the earth. 2982-4

"Ask and ye shall receive. Knock and it shall be
opened unto you," see? and as the conditions arise,
keeping then, both, in that way and manner that is
holy and acceptable unto Him, the Giver of all good
and perfect gifts. The supply will come from that
storehouse that is of His building, for none will suffer in the following of that way that leads to life eternal. For the physical must be supplied with those
necessary elements of life and sustenance to be
able to comprehend, to gain, the full and unexplor-
able conditions of the spiritual force manifest in the
material world.
Be thou faithful, then, guided, guarded, directed,
by Him. 294-41

For this purpose ye came into this experience;
that ye might *glorify* that consciousness, that
awareness of His presence, of His Spirit abiding
with thee.
Ye give manifestations of same in the manner, in
the way in which ye measure that love to others
about thee day by day.
This do, and ye will know the truth—the truth
shall indeed make you free. Not condemning, not
finding fault here nor there at any of the experiences; knowing that God is, and that ye must, that

ye *will,* that ye *may*—and it is the glorious opportunity, the glorious promise to just be able to be kind, to be gentle, to be patient with thy fellow man day by day!

And the *assurance* comes within thy own self, for His promise is to meet thee in the tabernacle of thy own conscience. For as Jesus said, "Lo, the kingdom of heaven is within *you.*" 1348-1

John 16:25

Till now I have been using figures of speech; a time is coming when I shall no longer use figures, but tell you of the Father in plain words. (N.E.B.)

These things have I spoken unto you in proverbs: but the time cometh, when I shall no more speak unto you in proverbs, but I shall show you plainly of the Father. (A.V.)

I have said this to you in figures; the hour is coming when I shall no longer speak to you in figures but tell you plainly of the Father. (C.B.)

John 16:26-27

When that day comes you will make your request in my name, and I do not say that I shall pray to the Father for you for the Father loves you himself, because you have loved me and believed that I came from God. (N.E.B.)

At that day ye shall ask in my name: and I say not unto you, that I will pray the Father for you: for the Father himself loveth you, because ye have loved me, and have believed that I came out from God. (A.V.)

In that day you will ask in my name; and I do not
say to you that I shall pray the Father for you; for
the Father himself loves you, because you have
loved me and have believed that I came from the
Father. (C.B.)

John 16:28-30

I came from the Father and have come into the
world. Now I am leaving the world again and going
to the Father. His disciples said, "Why, this is plain
speaking; this is no figure of speech. We are certain
now that you know everything, and do not need to
be questioned; because of this we believe that you
have come from God." (N.E.B.)

I came forth from the Father, and am come into the
world: again, I leave the world, and go to the Father. His disciples said unto him, Lo, now speakest
thou plainly, and speakest no proverb. Now we are
sure that thou knowest all things, and needest not
that any man should ask thee: by this we believe
that thou camest forth from God. (A.V.)

I came from the Father and have come into the
world; again, I am leaving the world and going to
the Father. His disciples said, Ah, now you are
speaking plainly, not in any figure! Now we know
that you know all things, and need none to question you; by this we believe that you came from
God. (C.B.)

John 16:31-33

Jesus answered, "Do you now believe? Look, the
hour is coming, has indeed already come, when

you are all to be scattered, each to his home, leaving me alone. Yet I am not alone, because the Father is with me. I have told you all this so that in me you may find peace. In the world you will have trouble. But courage! The victory is mine; I have conquered the world." (N.E.B.)

Jesus answered them, Do ye now believe? Behold, the hour cometh, yea, is now come, that ye shall be scattered, every man to his own, and shall leave me alone: and yet I am not alone, because the Father is with me. These things I have spoken unto you, that in me ye might have peace. In the world ye shall have tribulation: but be of good cheer; I have overcome the world. (A.V.)

Jesus answered them, Do you now believe? The hour is coming, indeed it has come, when you will be scattered, every man to his home, and will leave me alone; yet I am not alone, for the Father is with me. I have said this to you, that in me you may have peace. In the world you have tribulation; but be of good cheer, I have overcome the world. (C.B.)

So long as ye are in the earth, as He gave, there are tribulations to be experienced. But in the ideal—in spirit, in mind, in activity—we find that He overcame the world.

Within the experience of self, then, as ye choose— with those activities which come about thee, know Who and What is thy ideal.

As the warnings have been given of old, try ye the spirits, and they that are not of Him will declare themselves—just as they that are with him will do also. But by their fruits ye shall know them. For, with what measure ye mete it shall be measured to thee again; or with what measure they have meted, with that alone can and will they measure to thee again.

His promises are sure in man's experience. He gave, "I have overcome the world. Greater things ye shall do, or may do, in my name; for I go to the Father and will ever make intercession for thee, that ye may know indeed the glory of being at peace one with another, and in accord—or aware of thy peace with thy Maker." 967-3

Hence the first injunction would be—Find within self what is thy desire and purpose. Not merely material—for the material things and material positions should be the outgrowth, the result; and not the whole purpose of an experience.

For they that love Him have the promise that they *shall* be clothed, they *shall* not want for food nor sustenance of the body.

Then, these supplied—as they may be in the experience—there should be a greater desire to so live that ye may constrain those whom ye meet day by day to glorify Him; not by precept alone, not by merely laudation, but by example; sowing those things in thy life that are as the fruits of the spirit— faith, hope, love, kindness, gentleness, patience, brotherly love. And if ye have these, ye are secure and safe in the promises of Him—who *is* the Prince of Peace—not of the world as the world knows the world, but He that *overcame* the world! And so may ye overcome the world—in His promises. 1971-1

5

The Gospel of John, Chapter 17

"For thou has made him sovereign over all mankind . . ." (John 17:2)

It is in this chapter that Jesus gives what has been called the Priestly Prayer. Jesus recognized that God had made Him sovereign or ruler over all people, something that's difficult for us to comprehend. If we were to look at this event from the perspective of our status as having been created by God, as was discussed earlier in the book, we would see ourselves probably communicating word-lessly, like in a dream, and we would understand that the Creative Forces and the entity we call Jesus were one in consciousness. But we have not yet comprehended how all this comes about.

What is humankind? The Book of John Research Group wrestled with this problem and came up with its picture of what kind of beings we are, that helps in our comprehension of this matter of sovereignty. "We are sparks of light in an ocean of light, thoughts in the mind of God. We are individual points of consciousness uniquely expressing the universal. Once an individual experiences self as a life extending beyond the confines of the physical body, there is no limit to the growth in awareness he (or she) might attain."

We are not simply physical bodies—never have been, as a matter of fact. We are individual entities, souls, expressing as human beings here on the planet Earth in a physical body. Our presence here is primarily to learn how to love—to follow Him who became the Way, to return to where creation came about, in another spiritual dimension—not a physical, three-dimensional environment.

If our journey started there, then it seems more reasonable that the power or sovereignty over the flesh would come from that original, spiritual Source, once it is established.

It seems, then, that we are under the rule of the power of creation itself, since the entity whom we call Jesus fulfilled His purpose by overcoming the powers of the earth, the ruler of this environment whom He called the Prince of this World, the earth forces.

In following this Path home, then, our emotions become involved in a war between darkness and light, for we always act from a foundation of attitudes and emotions coming from the manners in which we have instructed our unconscious minds in the past. We have acted peacefully or in anger, we have chosen constructive, helpful attitudes like what Paul in biblical passages called the fruits of the Spirit—or we have chosen those emotions which are known as the desires of our lower nature. A oneness comes when we are obedient to the higher forces of light, when we choose today whom we will serve in our daily walk through this life.

John 17:1-2

After these words Jesus looked up to heaven and said: "Father, the hour has come. Glorify thy Son, that the Son may glorify thee. For thou has made him sovereign over all mankind, to give eternal life to all whom thou hast given him." (N.E.B.)

These words spake Jesus, and lifted up his eyes to heaven, and said, Father, the hour is come; glorify thy Son, that thy Son also may glorify thee: as thou hast given him power over all flesh, that he should give eternal life to as many as thou hast given him. (A.V.)

When Jesus had spoken these words, he lifted up his eyes to heaven and said, Father, the hour has come; glorify thy Son that the Son may glorify thee, since thou hast given him power over all flesh, to give eternal life to all whom thou hast given him. (C.B.)

John 17:3

This is eternal life; to know thee who alone are truly God, and Jesus Christ whom thou has sent. (N.E.B.)

And this is life eternal, that they might know thee the only true God, and Jesus Christ, whom thou has sent. (A.V.)

And this is eternal life, that they know thee the only true God, and Jesus Christ whom thou hast sent. (C.B.)

What *Is* Eternal Life?

When I was much younger, I pondered the idea of how anything could be without beginning and without end. That's how the dictionary defines the word *eternal*. I knew, of course, that each individual in the earth dimension is born here and dies here. Definitely not eternal, or at least it seemed so. But God is in another dimension, yet closely related to the earth and all its inhabitants.

I realized, somewhere along the way, that the earth, in fact, is not a three-dimensional structure—or, if it is, it certainly does not reside in a three-dimensional space. If I were to go straight out in space, I reasoned, I could never reach the end of space. The end would be butted up against more space, or another space, or more galaxies, or whatever. Perhaps geniuses like Albert Einstein could give an explanation detailing the nature of eternity.

Then, in my studies, I came across the second and third verses of John 17. "For thou has made him sovereign over all mankind, to give eternal life to all whom thou hast given him. This is eternal life; to know thee who alone are truly God, and Jesus Christ whom thou has sent." (N.E.B.)

This became another mystery. For how could one gain eternal life simply by "knowing" that power we call God? Then I caught the middle of that quote: Jesus had just asked God to glorify Him, so that He might "give eternal life to all whom thou hast given him."

This, for me, indicated a gift that Jesus was giving each of us, as souls—a gift simply of knowing God and knowing the Christ. But Jesus had to show us the Way. And He became the Way, by living it.

The picture appeared a bit clearer when I read this direct answer that Cayce gave to a man who had requested many readings. His questions were always searching for the truth. He simply asked, "What is meant by Life Eternal?" The answer:

Life Eternal—One with that Oneness, as is seen by the Soul becoming One with the Will, the Spirit, of the Father, even as is shown in the ensample of the Man called Jesus—the Christ, the Savior of the World, through compliance to those same laws, as He complied with, see? for with that Force, that Spirit, brought in the world, [it] then becomes the truth, "What thou asketh in My name, believing in thine heart, same shall be unto thee." *Beautiful* is the life and the feet of those who walk in the paths of the righteous One. Lo! The Heavens open and I see Him stand at that Way which leads unto Life Everlasting; *that* [is] then the Way, the Truth, the Light, the Water of Life, the Man made Perfect in that Spirit of Him who gave Himself as the ransom for many. In this is the ransom then: Making self of low estate, as is called in man's realm. All powerful—yet never using that power, save to help, to assist, to give aid, to give succor to someone who is not in that position to help or aid self, see? 900-147

There are laws, then, as govern the physical, the mental, the spiritual body, and the attributes of each of these. The abuse of a physical law brings dis-ease and then disturbance to the physical organism, through which mental and spiritual portions of the body operate.

There are also promises, warnings, and governing forces, as has been indicated, for the physical and the mental and spiritual being—as given by

those forces and influences which manifest in the
material world as respecting each of these.

As the Mind indicated, "I and the Father are one;
he that abideth in me as I abide in the Father *hath*
eternal life." Not *will* have, not *may* have, but
hath—now—is in eternal consciousness of being at
a onement with eternal influence and force! 1947-3

John 17:4

**I have glorified thee on earth by completing the
work which thou gavest me to do. (N.E.B.)**

**I have glorified thee on the earth: I have finished
the work which thou gavest me to do. (A.V.)**

**I glorified thee on earth, having accomplished the
work which thou gavest me to do ... (C.B.)**

These become self-evident facts in themselves,
or should, to those who apply themselves: Belief in
God, belief in self, belief in the divinity of man's relationship to God, accomplished for, by and through
one, Jesus the Christ. The belief, the faith, the doing
of that thy hands find to do which is in accord with,
in compliance with His desires, gives reason, gives
purpose, accomplishes that. For what were His
words? "Father, I come to thee, I have finished the
work thou gavest me to do." Hast thou finished the
work He gave thee to do; hast thou sought to know
the work? Hast thou walked and talked with Him
oft? It is thy privilege. Will ye? 3051-7

John 17:5

And now, Father, glorify me in thy own presence

with the glory which I had with thee before the
world began. (N.E.B.)

And now, O Father, glorify thou me with thine own
self with the glory which I had with thee before the
world was. (A.V.)

... and now, Father, glorify thou me in thine own
presence with the glory which I had with thee before the world was made. (C.B.)

Glorified Before the World Began

Before the world was created, Jesus was part of our
destiny. From these four chapters in the Book of John
and also in the Edgar Cayce readings, life is found to be a
continuous experience. We were there, too, before the
world was created, and we have experienced lifetime after lifetime seeking to find our way back to oneness with
God.

But what did Jesus mean when He spoke of "the glory
I had with the Father before the world was"? Cayce replied to the question by saying that it was "The opportunities; as Glory is only the means of opportunities for
expressing that purpose, that duty, that love, that law
which is before each soul." (262-94)

If Jesus was glorified in God's presence with the glory
which He had with God before the world began, then He
achieved that status in other dimensions. Given the
power to become the Savior of those on the earth, He
finally had to take part in the earth activities and overcome the earth Himself in order to show others the Way.
For, in truth, prior to His making love a reality in the
earth, none really knew what sin was—what lack of love
really meant to those of us dwelling in the earth.

Cayce gave a young lady, thirty-two years old, some

very important advice: "*Do not* attempt to justify self,
ever. Rather let thy purpose, thy desire, thy hope, thy
faith, ever be—in purpose—to the glory of the Father
through the Son, manifested in the earth, who *never—
never*—attempted to supplant; only applied the laws of
God in the spiritual, in the mental, and thus in the material brought miracles, the increase, the activity that overcame the laws of gravity. These *ye* may do, as the children
of God. For to each that lives with and in keeping with
the purposes of all to the glory of the Father, He gives
power for such to become the children of God, brothers
then with that way and purpose." (2390-7)

It seems to have been repeated over and over again
that the only way a concept concerning the nature of
humankind and of God can be made real is to have it
lived by an individual in the earth. Perfect love, then,
which in itself is complete attunement with the Creative
Forces of the Universe—God—had to be manifested in
human form in the earth to make it real. For that purpose, Jesus was born as a man, although He had already
been "glorified" by the Father in the spiritual realms. In
that manner, then, through that birth, it, the life lived,
became a reality, and humankind was given a measure,
a yardstick, by which all other activities might be measured. This means activities, feelings, attitudes, emotions, relationships—all of life can be seen measured up
against the magnitude of that way of living the law, the
law of love, the law of God, that we call the Christ Consciousness.

Cayce added to these thoughts, these concepts in
reading 262-115:

And these then show the mercy and the Patience
that He gives forth to each soul in this speck, this
dot in the universe. Yet He would have each soul,
each one of us, to become even as He—even as He

prayed: "Father, may they be with me where I am; that they may behold the glory I had with thee before the foundations of the world."

What do these words mean to us? That the Spirit has quickened us, so that we seek to manifest what? His mercy, His grace, His Patience among our fellow men.

It seems, too, that as we live a life fashioned after the Christ, we take steps toward being glorified in the eyes of the Creator—steps that we might understand as being on the path of spiritual growth. For this kind of a life glorifies God's presence within us by our living that love.

In summing up that which has been given respecting the manner in which individuals should apply themselves in relationships to activities for the *Glory* of the Father through the Son in their activities with and to their fellow man, we find:

The activities should come to be less and less for self, but more and more that self may be the channel through which the Glory of the Father may be manifested in the earth.

Then, the activities of self become less and less towards the Glory of self, less that good may come to thee. For being one with the Father, even as He has given, "As ye abide in me and I in the Father," then there may be that Glory, that consciousness of the oneness that thou didst occupy before thy advent or before the world was. Even as He prayed, "Now, glorify thy son, that he may have the glory that was his before the worlds were."

Hence, be—individuals in this group—as individuals preparing others that they, too, may know that Glory in their activities, in their lives. Not unto the Glory of self that thou may be only well-spoken of; for they that do such have indeed their own reward within their *earthly* experience. But they that do service *in* His name, for the Glory of the Father, may indeed know the Glory the Lord hath prepared for them that serve Him.

Quit ye yourselves like the children of the Father, knowing that His love, His Glory, abideth with those who love His ways, that keep His commandments, that *Glory* in the Cross and in a service to their fellow man. 262-93

Keep ye in touch with Him in thy purpose, in thy heart, in thy mind. For He hath loved thee and hath promised that He will come and abide with thee. He will bring that to thee that will give thee the more perfect understanding of that estate He had with the Father before the world was, before those experiences in the earth. And He will bring peace, harmony, understanding, glory in thy own experience. For though the heavens and the earth may pass away, though that thou hast builded in thy material world may appear to come to naught, though thy friends may forsake thee, though the very few may be in thy own experience as faithful, yet art thou faithful? Hast thou kept the way? Thinketh thou it were easy that those kept not awake for one hour, when the cares of the world, the experiences of unjustness were being piled upon Him? When ye because of a harsh word, a seeming unjustness have turned against this or that individual, when ye have separated thyself, when ye feel a hardship against another, think of thy Master. Then ye may indeed know that His promises are sure. For He hath borne the blame of the world upon His mind, His body *in the flesh;* yet He hath promised to stand between thee and those things that would make thee afraid.

For the way is easy when ye look to Him. Be ye joyous then in the fact, in the truth, in the knowledge, in the understanding that *thy* Brother, thy Savior, would be, will be, *is* nigh unto thee when ye pray, when ye seek that help, aid, health and harmony may be in the experience of thy neighbor. 281-27

Then indeed may there be a glimpse of the love the Father hath shown to the children of men, through the very gift of Him, thy Brother, the Christ; that we may walk circumspectly one with another; and thus give, show forth, *His* activity in the earth till we be made as one with Him, in the glories that were His and that are as He has given for us. For we be joint heirs, as one with Him; not strangers, not aliens but joint heirs with the Christ to the kingdom of the Father—that is, that was, that ever shall be—even before the foundations of the earth were laid. 1504-1

Sometime, somewhere, every soul meets that which itself, has been—good or bad. It is dependent, then, upon the choices; knowing thyself to be thyself, which only may be done in Him. For, as He sought, as He asked, "Father—that I may have that glory with thee that I had before the world was—that where I am there these may be also." The world then is indeed His, and all that in it is. Then walk, then think, then talk in that world of His—but be a citizen of that world that will be in honor and glory to Him—if ye would know thy [lost son] again. 3307-1

An experience through the earth's plane is for the development of the soul and not mere chance, nor is there no rule, no law that governs same. And the applications of the spiritual laws are just as definite and *more* true and more sure than those of material orders or material experiences of a material life.

For as in the material or secular world or rule there are those causes and effects, there are then *principles;* or an ideal as from which *all* such are judged. And so in the spiritual, in the mental, there are ideals. And these are constructive, and they be founded in those things that are as promises in the experience of man; which begin with, "If ye will be my people, I will be thy God—As the man in his experience soweth, so shall he reap—I have made thee a little lower than the angels, that ye might be through thy choice, through thy activity, not only purged from evil influence, evil thought, questionable conditions or experiences, but that ye might be one with me, that ye might know that glory that ye had *with* me before the worlds were."

And thus do those influences come in the experiences of each soul. 1217-1

John 17:6

I have made thy name known to the men whom thou didst give me out of the world. They were thine, thou gavest them to me, and they have obeyed thy command. (N.E.B.)

I have manifested in thy name unto the men which thou gavest me out of the world: thine they were, and thou gavest them me; and they have kept thy word. (A.V.)

I have manifested in thy name to the men whom thou gavest me out of the world; thine they were, and thou gavest them to me, and they have kept thy word. (C.B.)

John 17:7

Now they know that all thy gifts have come to me from thee ... (N.E.B.)

Now they have known that all things whatsoever thou hast given me are of thee. (A.V.)

Now they know that everything that thou hast given me is from thee ... (C.B.)

John 17:8

... for I have taught them all that I learned from thee, and they have received it: they know with certainty that I came from thee; and they have had faith to believe that thou didst send me. (N.E.B.)

For I have given unto them the words which thou gavest me; and they have received them, and have known surely that I came out from thee, and they have believed that thou didst send me. (A.V.)

... for I have given them the words which thou gavest me, and they have received them and know in truth that I came from thee; and they have believed that thou didst send me. (C.B.)

Remembering His mercy, remembering His prayer as He gave, "Yea, Father, that they may be one, even as I and Thou art one, that the world may know that Thou didst *send* me."

Wilt thou choose then, wilt thou not come as He has chosen each of you, to be a light to those that sit in darkness? Thus He may through thy feeble efforts (as they appear to thee, though in the power of His might they may) move mountains of doubt and fear in the hearts of those that are crying—crying that they may know the Lord, that they may understand the knowledge of God.

For the way is open, even to thee, my beloved. Faint not for doubts that arise. For He, the Savior, is thy strength, is thy power, yea *thy knowledge,* if ye will be *empty* thyselves of those secular forces that have made and do make for differences . . . 262-96

John 17:9-10

I pray for them; I am not praying for the world but for those whom thou has given me, because they belong to thee. All that is mine is thine, and what is thine is mine; and through them has my glory shone. (N.E.B.)

I pray for them: I pray not for the world, but for them which thou hast given me; for they are thine. And all mine are thine, and thine are mine; and I am glorified in them. (A.V.)

I am praying for them; I am not praying for the world but for those whom thou hast given me, for they are thine; all mine are thine, and thine are mine, and I am glorified in them. (C.B.)

John 17:11

I am to stay no longer in the world, but they are still in the world, and I am on my way to thee. Holy Father, protect by the power of thy name those whom thou has given me, that they may be one, as we are one. (N.E.B.)

And now I am no more in the world, but these are in the world, and I come to thee. Holy Father, keep through thine own name those whom thou hast given me, that they may be one, as we are. (A.V.)

And now I am no more in the world, but they are in the world, and I am coming to thee. Holy Father, keep them in thy name, which thou hast given me, that they may be one, even as we are one. (C.B.)

Let that desire, that thought, that purpose, be in each of you that was in the *Man* Jesus that, though He were in the world yet not of the world, neither was He strange nor curious, neither did He [refrain] from partaking of those things that were about Him in the social, in the home life of His fellow man. Yet His desire ever, "Not my will but Thine, O Lord, be done in me." As He has given ye, ye have all been called unto a service in Him; some to sacrifice here, others to toil and to disappointments there, yet He has promised and is able to keep that He has committed unto thy keeping against any obstacle, whether of the earth or of the unseen activities, against *thou* fulfilling that whereunto thou hast been called, if—*if*—thy *desire* is in Him. 262-70

For, as there may be builded in the heart and experience of those that act in the way to give those that come into the home (those of the body, as well as those of the physical and material associations) the place that is to represent that passing between the materiality and that whereunto He has called all that they be one with Him, so may the entity in this experience in the present bring for self—and for those whom the entity may contact—the greater blessings during this present experience. 524-1

What About the One That Must Be Lost,
the Son of Perdition?

Early in the thirteenth chapter of the Book of John, it's recorded that Jesus recognized what lay before Him and knew that Judas was going to betray Him, for He knew Scripture had to be fulfilled. He told His disciples, feeling deeply in His heart the pain that He knew was destined for His physical body, "In truth, in very truth I tell you, one of you is going to betray me." (Matt. 26:21)

Then, during this prayer for His disciples, in the last of these four discourses that were given for those who had followed Him so closely, there came this twelfth verse:

John 17:12

When I was with them, I protected by the power of thy name those whom thou has given me, and kept them safe. Not one of them is lost except the man who must be lost, for Scripture has to be fulfilled. (N.E.B.)

While I was with them in the world, I kept them in thy name: those that thou gavest me I have kept, and none of them is lost, but the son of perdition; that the scripture might be fulfilled. (A.V.)

While I was with them, I kept them in thy name, which thou hast given me; I have guarded them, and none of them is lost but the son of perdition, that the scripture might be fulfilled. (C.B.)

Perdition is not a word in common usage today, but as recently as the 1960s when the New English Bible was first published, *perdition* was accepted as a valid concept, a word worthy of use. *Webster* defines it as "Entire loss; ruin; esp., utter loss of the soul, or loss of final happiness in a future state; damnation." It is also defined in other sources as eternal damnation or hell.

Today hell is often commonly thought of as experiencing the trials and tribulations we often find ourselves facing here on earth. Especially is this true among many who do not understand or accept the idea of reincarnation and karma, which would explain that what we experience here is of our own making. There are those who believe in the "hellfire and damnation" destiny, as a place in reality for those who are not "believers." Yet there are still others who feel—or believe—that hell is simply a state of consciousness, whatever the cause may be. There is really no widely accepted definition as to what perdition or hell or damnation might be. Yet we have it as part of our Christian heritage, part of the Bible.

The Son of Perdition is another matter. In this seventeenth chapter of John, Jesus clearly identified Judas as having earned this title. Paul, in his second letter to the Thessalonians, described the Day of the Lord as not happening until the man doomed to perdition (or the Son of Perdition) had his way. Following are the first four verses of this second chapter, New English Bible version:

"And now, Brothers, about the coming of our Lord Jesus Christ and his gathering of us to himself; I beg you, do not suddenly lose your heads or alarm yourselves, whether at some oracular utterance, or pronouncement, or some letter purporting to come from us, alleging that the Day of the Lord is already here. Let no one deceive you in any way whatever. That day cannot come before the final rebellion against God, when wickedness will be revealed in

human form, the man doomed to perdition. [The
Authorized Version holds on to the term Son of Perdition.] He is the Enemy. He rises in his pride
against every god, so called, every object of men's
worship, and even takes his seat in the temple of
God claiming to be a god himself."

Let us always remember that, with each of us, our
body is the temple of God.

So, how do we best understand these words spoken
some two thousand years ago? Edgar Cayce's answer to
such a question sheds some light on it and gives us some
suggestions for our consideration:

Q. Explain John 17:12—"and none of them is lost,
but the son of perdition." What is meant by lost in
this sense, and just what would be meant by saved?

A. He had chosen rather to seek his *own* ways and
to deceive others into seeking to follow their own
manner rather than that there should be credence
or credit or loyalty or love shown to that source from
which life, consciousness or manifestations ema-
nated.

Hence that spoken of him that rebelled against
the throne of heaven, and manifested in the flesh in
the one who betrayed Him.

Then, all are sons of perdition—or allow that
force to manifest through them—who deny Him, or
who betray Him, or who present themselves to be
one thing and—under earthly environment or for
personal gain, or for reasons of gratification—do
otherwise; for they do but persecute, deny, betray
Him. 262-93

It appears, from the perspective of the Cayce readings,
that the Son of Perdition is that entity (created by God as

a son) who rebelled, in all of his power against the Throne of Heaven, against the Creative Forces of the Universe, God the Father, the Maker of all things. Jesus called him the Prince of this world. He was known as the Serpent, Satan, the old Devil, the Tempter, the power of darkness, of trouble, turmoil, strife, dissention, disorder, inharmony, and such (see 288-27).

The rebellion against the oneness of God, who *is* Love—this is the meaning of the Son of Perdition. It points out to us that we, as souls also created by God, have been given the power of choice "as to whether [we] will be one with the Father or, even as the son of perdition, attempt to establish self in glory of self." (262-118)

So perhaps we could say that the Son of Perdition is lost—he had to be separated from the face of the Father, for this is one of the mysteries of life in its manifestation, that the Scripture must be fulfilled.

But it also creates the battleground between the forces of light and the powers of darkness. Jesus manifests the love, the light of the Father, and as we move to follow in His footsteps, do as He did, we move into light and away from the darkness. As we with the same tongue bless God and yet in other ways deny Him for our own selfish purposes, we are to a degree, then, allowing ourselves to be guided by the same Force that denied Jesus and sent Him to the cross.

We can seek out the mysteries of life as it manifests itself in the earth, and do so with the desire that none shall be lost, but that all should approach and know the saving grace in the Lamb that takes away the sins of the world (see 452-6). This is one of the paths that leads to the light.

But we also have the right to seek for the mysteries that are preserved only for those who have conducted themselves in the manners to be worthy of the knowledge of those mysteries. This might be called the path of the higher calling. It may only be done by *being* kind, gentle, patient, and long-suffering when relationships from outside, events of the day tend to upset us. We take what we have in hand, which is our choice, and we love one another. In that way, we even overcome our karma from sojourns, past or present. We *can* reject the attempt to establish ourselves in glory of self. But, if we need help, which we usually do, we can support our efforts always by praying as one of the readings suggested:

"Father, keep Thou my mind, my heart open to thy calls! May I choose ever the spirit of the Christ to be the author of my activities day by day. May I be patient and long-suffering. May I be gentle—yea, may I be humble. For without these, the very activity may become a stumbling block. Then, keep my heart pure. Renew the righteous spirit within me, O God! day by day! May I hear again, as in the days of yore, the voice of the Christ as He calls to men to *renew* their faith and *manifest* their love of God in their dealings with their fellow man.

"May I fill that purpose whereunto Thou hast called me into service in the vineyard of the Christ, and may I fill it with that spirit that He manifested when He gave, 'Father, I condemn them not—they know not what they do.' " 262-118

John 17:13

And now I am coming to thee; but while I am still in the world I speak these words, so that they may have my joy within them in full measure. (N.E.B.)

And now come I to thee; and these things I speak in the world, that they might have my joy fulfilled in themselves. (A.V.)

But now I am coming to thee; and these things I speak in the world, that they may have my joy fulfilled in themselves. (C.B.)

John 17:14

I have delivered thy word to them, and the world hates them because they are strangers in the world, as I am. (N.E.B.)

I have given them thy word; and the world hath hated them, because they are not of the world, even as I am not of the world. (A.V.)

I have given them thy word; and the world has hated them because they are not of the world, even as I am not of the world. (C.B.)

John 17: 15-16

I pray thee, not to take them out of the world, but to keep them from the evil one. They are strangers in the world, as I am. (N.E.B.)

I pray not that thou shouldest take them out of the world, but that thou shouldest keep them from the evil. They are not of the world, even as I am not of the world. (A.V.)

I do not pray that thou shouldst take them out of the world, but that thou shouldst keep them from the evil one. They are not of the world, even as I am not of the world. (C.B.)

They Are Strangers in the World, as I Am

As noted above, the Authorized Version of the Bible states that "They are not of the world, even as I am not of the world." Edgar Cayce said of these four chapters, "Let them be as words to *thee!*" (1614-1) In other words, if the disciples were not of this world, if they are strangers in the world, then, to be consistent, we also are strangers in the world and find ourselves in the same situation as the disciples. We can take to heart what Jesus said in this chapter as in the other three chapters, paying attention, too, to those comments offered by Cayce in the course of his over 14,000 readings, given mostly for individuals.

What does it mean to say we are strangers in the world? Perhaps part of the answer lies in the nature of our beginning and our eventual destiny. We were created to be companions and cocreators with God. That is our destiny, to gain that status. Part of the answer lies in the fact that God created us, gave us life, as souls in His image, with the ability to choose—even to deny Him. Our basic nature is spiritual both in our conception and our end-point. Would we not, then, feel at some time like we are indeed strangers in this environment, beautiful though it is? There are laws, however, both in the Spirit and in the world, and these need to be understood and followed.

In one of his discourses, Cayce approached several questions that touch on our visit here in the earth, whether or not we feel as if we are strangers. In this reading, he showed how a single individual, even though ill, may make it possible that those who care for that person may be glorified in their efforts to serve. Although the afflicted one may not realize it, he or she, too, in a wonderful way, serves. Cayce did not enlarge on the manner in which one would carry out one's part of the relationships, but it is obvious that that individual needs to be gentle, thankful, loving, and receptive of the help that is offered. This is what Cayce had to say, in part:

Hence we find to keep, to hold to those things as He gave in the beginning, "Subdue ye the earth—make ye then the laws thereof thy servants, not thy enemies"—this is saying only "Sin not; for ye that know sin and have fallen short must meet these in thyself." And only as He hath shown the way. Though He were in the world, He was not of the world; yet subject to the laws thereof, of materiality.

For His heart ached, yea His body was sore and weary; yea His body bled not only from the nail prints in His hands and feet but from the spear thrust into the heart of hearts! For the blood as of the perfect man was shed, not by reason of Himself but that there might be made an offering once for all; that then *ye* may know, ye in thine own self are not a burden to any.

For with thy mind, thy heart, ye may give much, much the more to those about thee in their ministry to thy physical weaknesses; that the very glory of Him may be manifested in their lives. 1504-1

Because we are in the earth at the present time, it does not mean that we must serve or join with the forces of earth consciousness, the Prince of this world. Rather, we need to remember that we are visitors here and must be attentive to the laws of the earth. But we serve a higher master—we may be in the world but not of the world—and those higher laws take precedence, much as might be understood more clearly in these readings that follow:

. . . there must be raised in each individual that consciousness of the indwelling, or—to put it in

material manner—the *superseding of* the Christ
Consciousness *in* that matter that would be healed,
whether by its injection by those that through co-
operation raise such vibrations in an individual, or
through that of one individual raising same in *self.*
So, all these receive their consideration, as has been
given—*to* whom ye speak, *how* ye speak, where,
when, and *how*—these *must all be* considered,
would one *not* become arrogant, would one *not* become self-centered, self-condemning. Self surren-
dering first, then raise the consciousness that will
supersede, will overcome—for only in *His* name
may the world and *its* environs be overcome; for, as
He overcame even death, so may *ye* in *His* name
overcome the ills that the flesh is heir to, through its
advent into a material world. "I am *not* of this world.
Ye are not of this world, if *ye* abide in me—but I may
only be *manifest* in the material world through
thine *own* raising of that consciousness. As I abide
in the Father, and ye abide in me, I in ye, ye in me,
we may bring that to pass *as* ye seek." 281-3

. . . seek in the mental mind the answer to all
questions that may be presented in the things that
may be thy experiences day by day, and have the
answer within self as thou prayest. Then lay this
answer before the Throne of grace, or mercy itself,
as thou would meditate within the chambers of
thine own heart, and the answer will be within self
as to the necessary step, the necessary things to per-
form to be rid of the warring of the flesh with the
spirit. While each body, each soul, in the flesh is
subject to the flesh, yet—as has been given of Him,
"Though ye may be in the world, ye may not be *of*
this world, if ye will but put your whole trust, your
whole love, your whole life, in His keeping." He will

not lead thee astray. He will guide, guard and direct thee, even as has been given, "He loveth every one and giveth his own life for those that will come to Him."

In the preparations, then, for these warrings within, as has been given, meet them step by step. That that is given thee put to use, for only in the use of that which is thine own may this grow, even as patience and mercy and love and endurance and tolerance. Putting them to use they become those bulwarks that prevent an interception from carnal forces or the spirits of an evil influence. For, these are helpless in His sight; for He is made Lord of all. 442-3

In adding to that which has been given, or in summing it all up, *know* that to *know* the Glory indeed is to—self—be a part of that Glory; that which would come through thy efforts. Not as an honor, but as thy honoring the Christ—for His name's sake. Not that ye may be well-spoken of or looked upon by the world as something set aside. Rather as He gave, "*in* the world but not *of* the world" yet manifesting that which becomes the Glory of the Father among the children of men. 262-94

. . . with the abilities to use that in hand day by day, that here a little, there a little, line upon line, precept upon precept, there may be added unto self that which will bring the more and more awareness of that soul's development for the purposes for which it came into this special realm of activity at this time.

For, being of the world and in the world, the activities of the soul do not necessarily partake of the world, but rather those things upon which the soul itself may feed and bring into its experience that which will bring the peace that passeth understanding in Him. 556-1

Come! Sing a joyful song unto thy Lord and thy Redeemer, who hath *strengthened* thee in the hours of trial, of test, of tribulation; for they that meet their troubles, their sorrows, with *joy* in the Name of the Lord shall not be troubled again. They that kick against the pricks find that they but entangle their own mental minds, their own consciousnesses in the turmoils of the flesh. Ye *live* in the flesh, yet be as He—in the world yet not *of* the world; for all strength, all power, all glory, all joy is given unto Him—for *He* has overcome, and ye may in Him overcome also. Count it rather as a blessing, rather as that thou art *chosen* that ye may in the name of thy Lord speak a kind word to those that are abrupt or cross with thee, and in so doing ye will heap the coals of judgment upon their consciousnesses; for ye are His and He is thine, if ye will hold to that thou hast chosen. 262-72

And these are one—the body, the mind, the soul—even as the Father, the Son, the Holy Spirit are one; these coordinating, these as a purpose fullness not for self, not for self-indulgence, not for self-glory, not for self-gratification alone, but that the glory of Him may be magnified—who has been and who is the beginning and the end of all things in thy experiences!

If these are kept, they will bring harmony and peace in thy relationships with the world and the dwellers therein.

Be then in the world, yet not of the world. 1641-1

John 17:17-20

Consecrate them by the truth; thy word is truth. As thou has sent me into the world, I have sent them into the world, and for their sake I now consecrate myself, that they too may be consecrated by the truth. But it is not for these alone that I pray, but for those also who through their words put their faith in me. (N.E.B.)

Sanctify them through thy truth: thy word is truth. As thou hast sent me into the world, even so have I also sent them into the world. And for their sakes I sanctify myself, that they also might be sanctified through the truth. Neither pray I for these alone, but for them also which shall believe on me through their word ... (A.V.)

Sanctify them in the truth; thy word is truth. As thou didst send me into the world, so I have sent them into the world. And for their sakes I consecrate myself, that they also may be consecrated in truth. I do not pray for these only, but also for those who believe in me through their word ... (C.B.)

Q. Just how can I gain a better or greater understanding and control of my peculiar attitude towards various individuals?

A. Look into self, and those eccentricities of thine own activity; and these may be studied better by studying nature, by studying the soil, the product of same, the varied activities as in things growing, as in the birds and the bees, as in the flowers, as in the trees, as in those things that live or act about thee. Keep *alone* for periods at a time. Let thyself make a study of these. And let much of the time be

spent in meditation and prayer. Read (not until they
become as rote, but as living words) the last words,
the last message as He gave, as thy Master gave, "In
my Father's house are many mansions; if it were not
so I would have told you. I go to prepare a way, that
where I am there you may be also. And I pray not
for these alone, but for those that may *through*
these know of Thee." 1089-3

John 17:21

May they all be one; as thou, Father, art in me, and
I in thee, so also may they be in us, that the world
may believe that thou didst send me. (N.E.B.)

... that they all may be one; as thou, Father, art in me,
and I in thee, that they also may be one in us: that
the world may believe that thou hast sent me. (A.V.)

... that they may all be one; even as thou, Father,
art in me, and I in thee, that they also may be in us,
so that the world may believe that thou hast sent
me. (C.B.)

John 17:22

The glory which thou gavest me I have given to
them, that they may be one, as we are one. (N.E.B.)

And the glory which thou gavest me I have given
them; that they may be one, even as we are one ...
(A.V.)

The glory which thou hast given me I have given to
them, that they may be one even as we are one.
(C.B.)

Q. What changes had to take place in the physical body of Jesus to become a glorified spiritual body?

A. The passing of the material life into the spiritual life brought the *glorified* body; thus enabling the *perfect* body to be materialized in material life—a *glorified* body made perfect! 5749-10

John 17:23

... I in them and thou in me, may they be perfectly one. Then the world will learn that thou didst send me, that thou didst love them as thou didst me. (N.E.B.)

... I in them, and thou in me, that they may be made perfect in one; and that the world may know that thou hast sent me, and hast loved them, as thou hast loved me. (A.V.)

I in them and thou in me, that they may become perfectly one, so that the world may know that thou hast sent me and hast loved them even as thou hast loved me. (C.B.)

John 17:24

Father, I desire that these men, who are thy gift to me, may be with me where I am, so that they may look upon my glory, which thou hast given me because thou didst love me before the world began. (N.E.B.)

Father, I will that they also, whom thou hast given me, be with me where I am; that they may behold my glory, which thou hast given me: for thou

lovedst me before the foundation of the world.
(A.V.)

Father, I desire that they also, whom thou hast
given me, may be with me where I am, to behold
my glory which thou hast given me in thy love for
me before the foundation of the world. (C.B.)

Let that mind ever be in thee as was in Him as He
offered Himself up: "Father, forgive them—they
know not what they do. Father, it is finished—I
come to Thee. Give Thou Thy servant that glory
which Thou hast promised."
Live that in thy life, thy conversation, thy activity
everywhere; and indeed then may each in that
manner bear a real Easter message to others.
For He hath entrusted to thee—those that love
Him—the redemption of the world, to make known
His willingness, His care, His promises that may be
the activity of each and every soul . . . Let thy light,
then, shine ever in the dark, in the light; in the sorrow, in the gladness of thy purpose, of thy desire;
that He may be glorified even as He asks of the Father. 5749-13

John 17:25

O righteous Father, although the world does not
know thee, I know thee, and these men know that
thou didst send me. (N.E.B.)

O righteous Father, the world hath not known thee:
but I have known thee, and these have known that
thou hast sent me. (A.V.)

O righteous Father, the world has not known thee,
but I have known thee; and these know that thou
hast sent me. (C.B.)

John 17:26

I made thy name known to them, and will make it
known, so that the love thou hadst for me may be
in them, and I may be in them. (N.E.B.)

And I have declared unto them thy name, and will
declare it; that the love wherewith thou hast loved
me may be in them, and I in them. (A.V.)

I made known to them thy name, and I will make it
known, that the love with which thou hast loved
me may be in them, and I in them. (C.B.)

The Light That Never Fails

"When all things began, the Word already was. The
Word dwelt with God, and what God was, the Word was.
The Word, then, was with God at the beginning; and
through him all things came to be; no single thing was
created without him. All that came to be was alive with
his life, and that life was the light of men. The light shines
on in the dark, and the darkness has never mastered it."
This quote, telling about the nature and presence of
Jesus in the spiritual realm and in the earth, comes from
verses 1-5 of the first chapter of the Gospel of John.

The perspective regarding spiritual matters as viewed
from the minds of earthly beings continues as a mystery
here. The Word is the Christ, who became known as Jesus
in this incarnation. And, as Cayce reminded us, He was
already with God before the earth came into being. And
it was through Him that all creation associated with the

earth came into being. In many references over the centuries, He became known as the Light That Never Fails.

Then, in His final prayer about His disciples, and
about us (if Cayce's insight is to be believed), Jesus asked
that this same power, the Love that God granted Him,
might be bestowed on each one of us. Perhaps it is in
this manner that we can bring light to the world through
our becoming instruments of God's love in the world.

The message here might be, in all instances, to help
those we can—our neighbor, our brother and sister,
those who are the seekers—to stand on their own two
feet, to live the life that tells of the Christ and His meaning to the whole world, as the light that never fails, the
way, the truth, the life itself which flows through our
bodies—to walk in His footsteps.

I had never truly realized before I read this next reading, 3976-15, that those who were "weaklings," those
who do not use their power to choose, who do not exercise that gift from God, will need to go through these
karmic experiences in lifetime after lifetime until they
learn.

The fact that Jesus did this—entered into the crucible
and became as naught—was His choice, having already
in other dimensions become glorified in God's sight; and
in this world, He overcame all the temptations that we
might face. He did it to bring love as a reality into the
world, allowing us to overcome our karma by doing it His
way, simply by loving.

Cayce told us that there are no karmic debts from this
or other sojourns that cannot be met in "Lord, have Thy
ways with me." His ways, of course, are simply loving
each other in all circumstances.

To be healed is to be freed from the confines of the
earth, the desires of the flesh, the search for self-gratification, and our confusion in the manner we live our lives
that has come to be called sin. He became the Light, the

Life, the Way, and the Pattern we need to follow to understand our origin and our destiny. The reading:

> . . . ye that sit here and that hear and that see a light breaking in the east, and have heard, have seen thine weaknesses and thine faultfindings, and know that He will make thy paths straight if ye will but live that *ye know* this day—then may the next step, the next word, be declared unto thee. For ye in your weakness have known the way, through that as ye have made manifest of the *spirit* of truth and light that has been proclaimed into this earth, that has been committed unto the keeping of Him that made of Himself no estate but who brought into being all that ye see manifest in the earth, and has declared this message unto thee: "Love the Lord thy God with all thine heart," and the second is like unto it, "Love thy neighbor as thyself." Who is thine neighbor? Him that ye may aid in whatsoever way that he, thy neighbor, thy brother, has been troubled. Help him to stand on his own feet. For such may only know the acceptable way. The weakling, the unsteady, must enter into the crucible and become as naught, even as He, that they may know the way. 3976-15

6

What Do We Do with This Man, Jesus?

"I have glorified thee on earth by completing the work which thou gavest me to do; and now, Father, glorify me in thy own presence with the glory which I had with thee before the world began." (John 17:4-5)

In these times, those who tell the story of Jesus often say, "If you believe, you will be saved; if you do not believe, you will go to hell." Others avoid the question of what to do with this Man. Some soften the answer; others walk away from the whole affair.

Most churches follow their traditions, their laws that do not allow for the concept that Jesus could have been incarnated here many times in order to fulfill the law of the Divine. Most avoid the idea of reincarnation. Nearly all Christian churches soft-pedal the idea that through Jesus—the eternal entity, Jesus—the world was created.

All these ideas and more came into my mind as I have been writing this book.

For I have asked myself, "What will you do with this Man, Jesus?" In the next few pages, I will share with you what I have done and will continue to do in answering this question. Then, I will invite—no, challenge—you to look inside yourself, ask from the point of consciousness within your special temple, and formulate what you want to do with that question—*what will you do with this Man, Jesus?*

Then, will you be willing to take what you understand Him to be into your life, into your interpersonal relationships, and follow His suggestions, walk in His footsteps?

Let's first explore my experiences. For, I cannot ask you a question if I have not already attempted an answer myself and tried to live that answer, knowing it is, at best, only a step toward that oneness that Jesus has already achieved.

How Do I See Jesus the Christ?

After working for a quarter of a century with the ideas found in the fourteenth through the seventeenth chapters of John—and the associated Edgar Cayce readings—I have written much in this book about Jesus. But I would like to review, perhaps summarize, what appears most prominently in my mind about this Man as I live my life from day to day.

Jesus was born of a virgin. His father was not Joseph, but rather the energy of the Holy Spirit, the power that gives all of us life.

From my training and background, I understand every conception, every beginning of new life in the womb of the mother as a miracle. It's part of the divine plan that allows human beings to inhabit the earth and to make it as their footstool. But we do not know how birth really comes about—we must be content with identifying genetic structures, or electrical impulses, or electromagnetic fields. We do not know what the magic is that allows one sperm to take precedence over thousands of others, penetrate the wall of the ovum, and bring about a special spark of union between two cells that says, "I am a new living being here waiting to be born." It happens so frequently that we accept it as the norm, but we do not understand the miracle.

In a like manner, a spark of divine, intelligent energy moved within Mary's womb and made it possible that Jesus could be conceived and then born as other individuals are born.

That was not the only remarkable event, however. While the child was being formed in utero, the Christ Himself left the spiritual realms and became part of the unborn child, making the two one—the God-Man. And Jesus' adventure had begun.

What is rarely understood, of course, is that this is His world that He was entering, one that He created. And *that* made Him special, entering on a divine mission. He chose to come into His own creation. Even those who were His did not know Him.

Having overcome the earth with its desires and wants, He gained the power to overcome gravity, to heal the sick, to bring the dead back to life, and to still the very elements. He could see—and know—all of the past and foretell the future—except where the willfulness of humankind may have altered the paths that could have been made straight. Then His dying on the cross completed His journey, fulfilled His purpose for being born—to make forgiveness and love real in the earth.

How can anyone summarize what Jesus' life has meant to the world and its inhabitants? But, the question remains:

What Do I Do with This Man, Jesus?

My answers to this question do not reflect a deep wisdom, I'm sure, nor the knowledge of the ages. My first response is to say that I believe that He existed and does exist today in a form that is much like the form of the Creator, since they are one. He can appear in the form that He had as Jesus, but He is part of each of us and is available within if we simply "open the door."

I believe what Jesus said. To believe otherwise would be to call Him a liar, and I'm not about to ever make that error. He said that He is the Way, the Truth, and the Life, and that no one cometh to the Father but by Him. I believe that, and I recognize that His way is a way of love, which I have written about earlier in this book. I also believe that I must, at some point in my existence, put that kind of love into action totally in my daily activities. I'm still working on that and have plenty of opportunities, since my karmic cup is still overflowing. But I know that I have been given a gift—a full forgiveness, when I accept it, covering all the problems (or opportunities) that I have ever brought into being. And I believe that Jesus made that forgiveness real when He experienced the crucifixion.

Jesus gave us a picture of God as loving, forgiving, joyful, and peaceful, and from my experiences and my reading and studying and trying to live these concepts, I find that which is of God is always good, constructive, and totally loving, with all the definitions that Paul in the Bible placed in context with love.

So, I accept the Christ as real, as my Elder Brother, the One who truly lets me understand that if I ask for anything, believing and acting in accord with my beliefs, then it will be given me. But above all, I see Jesus as the Christ, the Savior, who gave us—gave me—eternal life in a way that I still find hard to understand. But it is real.

Before I was as aware of things as I am at the present time, I failed to measure up as well to what God wants of me. No sense in listing the pitfalls—the list is too long for my comfort. But the overcoming of these mistakes has involved the love that Jesus talked about and has brought me closer to understanding something about forgiveness and what oneness really means. For, as my beginning was as a soul in the likeness of God, made in His image, my destiny is like unto my beginning—a oneness with Him, through the Path, the Way of the Christ Consciousness. I am destined, as you, to be a cocreator with the Divine.

Having answered my own question, I want to remind you that I have not taken you off the hook! I challenge you to answer for yourself, "What will you do with this Man, Jesus?" The last two Cayce readings that bring this book to a close will help you as you ponder.

For, in the Beginning was the Word, and that Spirit, that Christ Spirit *was* the Word. That Word was made flesh, even as each soul that manifests in the earth is made flesh. That soul, that spirit, *dwelt* among men, and that soul made itself of no estate; yet the Creator, the Maker, the Giver of the life itself; that man, that each soul, that this soul, might know that it has an advocate *with* the Father through Him that gave Himself as a ransom. How? For, as the impulses in self arise, know those impulses have arisen in Him; yet through the ability to overcome death in the material world is His presence able to abide with thee, dost thou trust in Him and not in self. Or, as He gave, in Him who *is* the Maker and the Creator is life alone, and they that put their trust in anything else climb up some other way. But they that put their trust in Him are His, and He calleth them by name, and He abideth with them. When ye call on Him He is very near.

Know, then, that in this experience thou mayest come to know Him as thine daily companion in whatsoever thou doest; for, "If ye love me, keep my commandments." What are His commandments? A new commandment He gave, that ye love one another, even as He hast loved thee. 524-2

For, all might, all power in heaven and in earth has been given into His keeping. For, He—having overcome the influences of the world of matter, being endowed with the spirit of truth, and helpfulness, and hopefulness, and love—is able to keep thee from falling into the errors of materiality or of ease.

But directing in those ways that make for the assurance of His abiding grace and mercy and strength, ye may present to thy fellow man—as ye are called on to do—an example, a way, a lesson; yet a weapon that will bring to others peace, harmony, and the longing for the filling of their lives—as well as thine own—with love and beauty and charm, that brings the consciousness of His abiding presence. 1877-1

A.R.E. PRESS

The A.R.E. Press publishes quality books, videos, and audiotapes meant to improve the quality of our readers' lives—personally, professionally, and spiritually. We hope our products support your endeavors to realize your career potential, to enhance your relationships, to improve your health, and to encourage you to make the changes necessary to live a loving, joyful, and fulfilling life.

For more information or to receive a free catalog, call

1-800-723-1112

Or write

A.R.E. Press
P.O. Box 656
Virginia Beach, VA 23451-0656

DISCOVER HOW THE EDGAR CAYCE MATERIAL CAN HELP YOU!

The Association for Research and Enlightenment, Inc. (A.R.E.®), was founded in 1931 by Edgar Cayce. Its international headquarters are in Virginia Beach, Virginia, where thousands of visitors come year round. Many more are helped and inspired by A.R.E.'s local activities in their own hometowns or by contact via mail (and now the Internet!) with A.R.E. headquarters.

People from all walks of life, all around the world, have discovered meaningful and life-transforming insights in the A.R.E. programs and materials, which focus on such areas as holistic health, dreams, family life, finding your best vocation, reincarnation, ESP, meditation, personal spirituality, and soul growth in small-group settings. Call us today on our toll-free number

1-800-333-4499

or

Explore our electronic visitor's center on the
INTERNET: **http://www.are-cayce.com**

We'll be happy to tell you more about how the work of the A.R.E. can help you!

> A.R.E.
> 67th Street and Atlantic Avenue
> P.O. Box 595
> Virginia Beach, VA 23451-0595